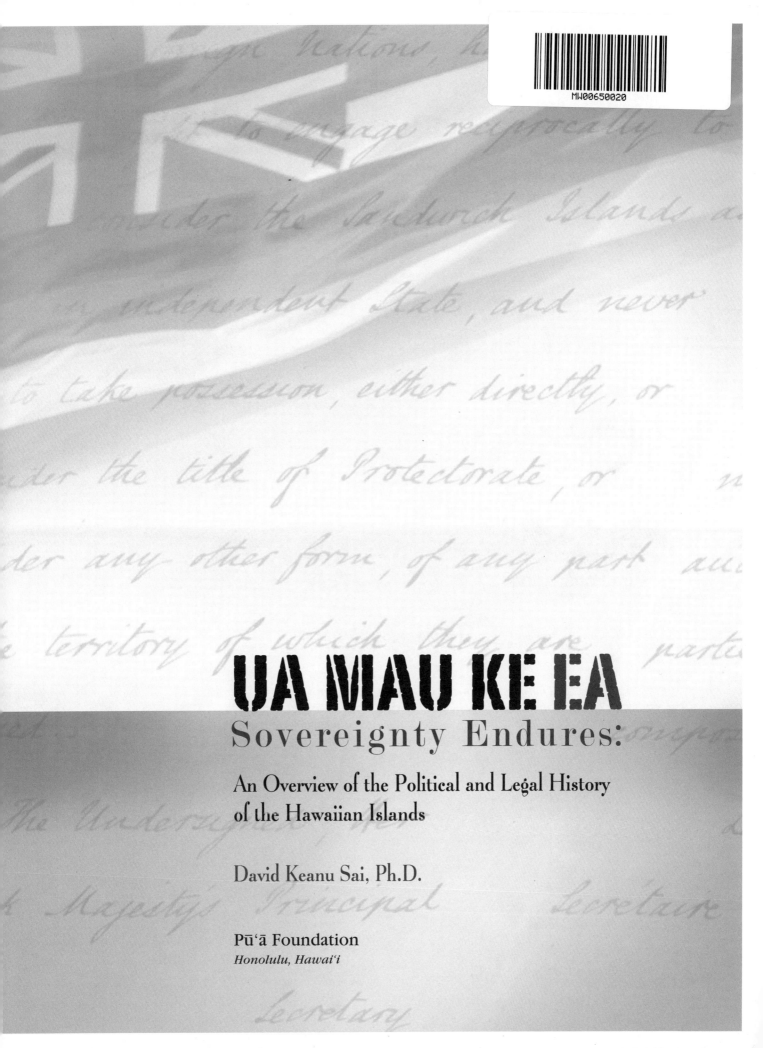

UA MAU KE EA

Sovereignty Endures:

An Overview of the Political and Legal History
of the Hawaiian Islands

David Keanu Sai, Ph.D.

Pūʻā Foundation
Honolulu, Hawaiʻi

Pūʻā Foundation

Book Design: PBR HAWAII & Associates, B. Kanaiʻa Nakamura

ISBN: 978-1-4507-8237-1

Printed in Hawaiʻi
July 2011

To Nani,

Aloha 'Āina

Ken

To Marji,

Aloha, Alive

Kai

UA MAU KE EA
Sovereignty Endures

CONTENTS

PREFACE

This publication and accompanying DVD were produced under Pū'ā Foundation's Hawaiian Historical Production Project. Through commissioned work and collaborative partnerships with the Hawai'i Research Institute led by David Keanu Sai, Ph.D. and Kau'i Sai Dudoit, Director of the Ho'olaupa'i Hawaiian Newspaper Project, these community educational resources assist in bringing about a deeper and clearer understanding of Hawai'i's history. The book is an extension of Dr. Sai's doctoral work, and with expertise drawn from Ms. Sai Dudoit's work with Hawaiian Newspapers, the DVD incorporates components of Hawaiian literacy. Proceeds from the sale of *Ua Mau Ke Ea* will support efforts to adapt these materials for other academic levels and as Hawaiian medium resource materials.

Pū'ā Foundation is a 501(c)(3) non-profit organization that was established in 1996 as part of the apology, redress, and reconciliation initiatives of the United Church of Christ and the Hawaiian people for the Church's complicity in the 1893 overthrow. Through dialogue and healing, great things are possible. It's not about changing minds, it's about changing hearts. The Foundation's vision is that through *pū'ā*, the process of feeding, nourishing and strengthening, enlightened and empowered communities and society will emerge. Through three core programs: 1) Research Development, 2) Product Development, and 3) Forum/Dialogue Development, the Foundation seeks to create opportunities to learn together, work together, and eat together so that there can be reconciliation of the past to the present and that together as a Hawai'i community, a better future can be built. These community educational resources of the Hawaiian Historical Production Project were developed under these programs. To learn more go to *www.puafoundation.org*.

ACKNOWLEDGMENTS

There are so many to thank. To begin – *Mahalo nui i ke akua, i nā 'aumakua, i nā kūpuna, a me ko'u 'ohana* – it is an honor that we are able to shine the light on the brilliance of those who came before us.

Special thanks go out to the current and former Board of Directors of the Pū'ā Foundation for their dedication and commitment to the Hawaiian Historical Production Project, an effort many years in development – Mark Kawika Patterson, Lei Kapono, Roberta Jahrling, Kealahou Alika, Stanley Lum, Aletha Kaohi, Puanani Burgess and Hamilton McCubbin.

Great appreciation for their hard work and contributions are extended to Jiggy Sai, Cecilia Perry, Marti Steele, Puakea Nogelmeier, Ph.D, Nahua Patrinos, Ph.D, Doris Miocinovic, and Audrey Enseki Tom.

For the layout and design work, thank you to B. Kanai'a Nakamura, creative director at PBR Hawai'i & Associates and mahalo nui loa for the financial support provided by a grant from Kamehameha Publishing, headed by Kehau Abad, Ph.D.

Moreover, this project would not have been possible without the scholarly work of Dr. Keanu Sai and the efforts of Kau'i Sai Dudoit, whose leadership and dedication were above and beyond the call. Words cannot express my utmost appreciation for all they have done.

It has been an honor and a privilege to work with so many special people who have been a part of developing these materials. As in life, it's all a process and the process that went into developing the book and DVD was a journey, with many ups and downs, but the important thing is that you always keep on going along the path. So from all of us, thank you for perusing the pages of the book and for viewing the video. May you receive it as the makana it is meant to be.

Me Ke Aloha - Toni Bissen – *Executive Director, Pū'ā Foundation*

INTRODUCTION

*I*n the latter part of the eighteenth century, the archipelago of the Hawaiian Islands consisted of four distinct kingdoms: Hawai'i under Kamehameha I; Maui with its dependent islands of Lāna'i and Kaho'olawe under Kahekili; Kaua'i and its dependent island of Ni'ihau under Kā'eo;[1] and O'ahu with its dependent island of Moloka'i under Kahahana. Kamehameha, King of Hawai'i Island, consolidated the four kingdoms establishing the Kingdom of the Sandwich Islands in 1810, which later became the Kingdom of the Hawaiian Islands.[2] The kingdom shared a similar language, religion, culture, and genealogy of the other Polynesian people of the South Pacific.

Historians speculate that between 1 and 300 A.D., Polynesians migrated from the Marquesan Islands and settled the islands of the North Pacific. Settlers from the Society Islands arrived later and stayed until the 14th century. These cultures were advanced and complex, with a monarchy, a political bureaucracy, a tax collection custom, a religious structure, and a stratified social system.[3] It was common practice for chiefs to leave one court and be accepted by another. Chiefs usually were forced to move from one court to another due to royal disfavor or failed rebellion. The commoner class was not as transient as the chiefs, but lived on the lands of a chief, in a society similar to the feudal system that prevailed in Europe during the Middle Ages.[4]

British East India Company flag, circa 1820

Kamehameha governed his kingdom according to ancient tradition and strict religious protocol. In 1794, after voluntarily ceding the island Kingdom of Hawai'i to Great Britain, Kamehameha and his chiefs considered themselves British subjects and recognized King George III as emperor. The cession to Great Britain did not radically change traditional governance, but principles of English governance and titles were instituted. Kamehameha adopted a national flag design very similar to the British East India Company with the same Union Jack in the canton, but replaced the thirteen red and white stripes with seven alternating colored stripes of white, blue and red to signify the seven major Islands.[5] The eighth Island kingdom of Kaua'i was a vassal kingdom under Kamehameha through voluntary cession by its King, Kaumuali'i, in 1810. An eighth stripe wouldn't be added to the national flag until May 25, 1845 when a revised national ensign was unfurled at the opening of the Hawaiian legislature.

By 1829, Kamehameha III and the Council of Chiefs began to exert Hawaiian autonomy from British rule. Both France and the United States' strategic interest in the Islands precluded the British from asserting their sovereignty. Finally, on November 28, 1843, Kamehameha III achieved the formal recognition of the Hawaiian Islands as an independent and sovereign State by proclamation from Great Britain and France. And on July 6, 1844, the United States joined the British and the French in their formal recognition of the Hawaiian Islands as a sovereign State.[6]

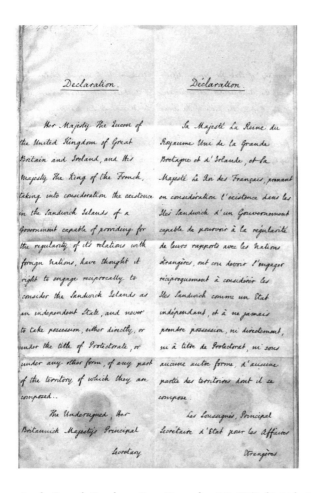 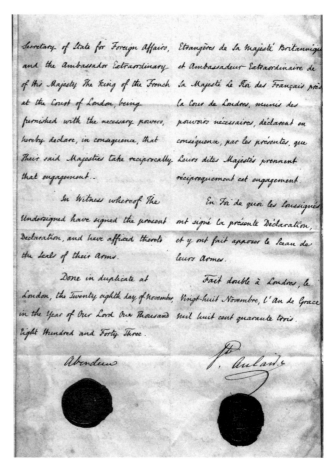

Anglo-French Proclamation, November 28, 1843 (British Archives)

Department of State,
Washington, July 6th. 1844.

Gentlemen.

The note which you did me the honor to address to me of date July 1st 1844. has been received and laid before the President, and in reply to it I am instructed to say that the communication heretofore addressed to you by the Secretary of State (Mr Webster) dated the 19th of December, 1842. with the Message of the President to Congress of the 31st of December, 1842, and the proceedings thereon of the House of Representatives, the appropriation made for the compensation of a Commissioner of the United States who was

To Messrs. T. Haalilio and Wm. Richards,
&c.   &c.   &c.

subsequently appointed to reside in the Sandwich Islands, were regarded by the President as a full recognition on the part of the United States, of the Independence of the Hawaiian Government. This opinion has undergone no change; and as the course adopted by the Government of the United States in this conforms substantially with the rule by which it has been regulated in all similar cases, it does not appear to the President necessary to introduce any other or more formal mode of recognition.

I have the honor to be, Gentlemen, your obedient servant,

J. C. Calhoun

U.S. Recognition Letter by Secretary of State Calhoun, July 6, 1844 (Hawai'i Archives)

PART 1
Evolution of Absolute Rule

CHAPTER 1
THE RISE OF KAMEHAMEHA

The Kingdom of Hawai'i Island was governed by a mixture of religious and chiefly laws. Government was absolute with a highly defined hierarchy of chiefs. According to David Malo, a Hawaiian historian:

> *The king was the real head of the government; the chiefs below the king, the shoulders and chest. The priest of the king's idol was the right hand, the minister of interior (kanaka kālaimoku) the left hand, of the government. This was the theory on which the ancients worked. The soldiery were the right foot of the government, while the farmers and fishermen were the left foot. The people who performed the miscellaneous offices represented the fingers and toes.*[7]

The chiefs and priests as the King's agents were strictly obeyed by the commoners. The King was compared to a house, "the chiefs below him and the common people throughout the whole country were his defense."[8] The King and his principal chiefs in council dealt with political, social and religious issues, and laws or edicts. The religious laws both organized and stratified Hawaiian society, while the chiefly laws gave the King his authority:

> *As a general mark the chiefs were regarded as the only proprietors. They were admitted to own not only the soil but also the people who cultivated it; not only the fish of the sea but also the time, services, and implements of the fisherman. Everything that grew or had life on the land or in the sea; also things inanimate, and everything formed or acquired by the skill or industry of the people was admitted to be owned by the chiefs.*[9]

Hawaiian Chief (Hawai'i Archives)

King's Heiau (Hawai'i Archives)

The unwritten governance consisted of two basic *kānāwai* (laws), "the *kānāwai akua*, or gods' laws; and the *kānāwai kapu ali'i*, or sacred chiefly laws."[10] Religious laws were closely interwoven with chiefly laws and the King's duty was "to consecrate the temples, to oversee the performance of the religious rites in the temples of human sacrifice," and to preside over ceremonies.[11] Sovereignty was consolidated in the King, who controlled life and death and could unilaterally change the form of governance. Religion constituted the organic law of the country while, administratively, governance resided solely with the King and his chiefs. Hawaiian Justice Walter Frear noted:

> *The system of government was of a feudal nature, with the King as lord paramount, the chief as mesne lord and the common man as tenant paravail—generally three or four and sometimes six or seven degrees. Each held land of his immediate superior in return for military and other services and the payment of taxes or rent. Under this system all functions of government, executive, legislative and judicial, were united in the same persons and were exercised with almost absolute power by each functionary over all under him, subject only to his own superiors, each function being exercised not consciously as different in kind from the others but merely as a portion of the general powers possessed by a lord over his own.[12]*

When the King of Hawai'i, Kalani'opu'u, died in January of 1782, his son, Kīwala'ō, became his successor,[13] while Kamehameha became the successor to the war-god, Kūka'ilimoku.[14] According to tradition, all lands held by the chiefs of Kalani'opu'u would revert to Kīwala'ō for redistribution to his most trusted chiefs. Kīwala'ō's short reign was beset by turmoil and rebellion of the Kona chiefs, who were his father's former chiefs.

The Kona chiefs looked to Kamehameha for leadership because they feared losing their lands during the traditional *kālai'āina* or redistribution of lands by Kīwala'ō.[15] The Kona chiefs' loyalty to Kīwala'ō was tenuous and fighting broke out with the King's brother, Keōua, after Keōua led a raiding party into Kamehameha's territory, killing some of Kamehameha's people. When Keōua cut down coconut trees, a traditional symbol of war, he started a chain of events that would ultimately fracture the island kingdom.[16] The raid happened "without the command or sanction of Kīwala'ō," but the new King "was gradually drawn into it in support of his brother."[17] Thus began a civil war and the rise of Kamehameha and the Kona chiefs.

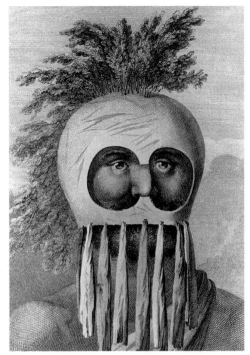

Masked Priest of War God Kūka'ilimoku
(Hawai'i Archives)

Both sides gathered their armies and engaged in an historic battle at Ke'ei in the district of Kona. At the onset of battle, known as the battle of *Moku'ōhai* [grove of 'ōhai trees], the Kona chiefs were suitably prepared for battle, but Kamehameha and his high priest were still performing a religious rite in preparation for the battle. It first appeared that Kīwala'ō would be victorious, until Kamehameha and his men joined the Kona chiefs, and the royal forces were finally defeated. A Kona chief, Ke'eaumoku, was severely wounded after he killed Kīwala'ō.[18] Kamehameha's army captured Kīwala'ō's chief counselor, Keawema'uhili, but Keōua, who instigated the battle, retreated with his army and took refuge in Ka'ū, the southern district of the island. Keawema'uhili later escaped to the windward side of the island. The battle of *Moku'ōhai* rendered:

> the island of Hawai'i into three independent and hostile factions. The district of Kona, Kohala, and portions of Hāmākua acknowledged Kamehemeha as their sovereign. The remaining portion of Hāmākua, the district of Hilo, and a part of Puna, remained true to and acknowledged Keawema'uhili as their Mō'ī [sovereign]; while the lower part of Puna and the district of Ka'ū, the patrimonial estate of Kīwala'ō, ungrudgingly and cheerfully supported Keōua Kū'ahu'ula against the mounting ambition of Kamehameha.[19]

Civil war continued for the next five years. Keawema'uhili and Keōua formed an alliance, and although they had skirmishes with Kamehameha, none was decisive enough to alter the balance of power established by the battle of *Moku'ōhai*. After Kamehameha's last campaign in 1785 against the Ka'ū and Hilo forces, Kamehameha returned to Kohala, "where he turned his attention to agriculture, himself setting an example in work and industry."[20] He also married Ka'ahumanu who would later become a prominent figure in modern Hawaiian history.[21]

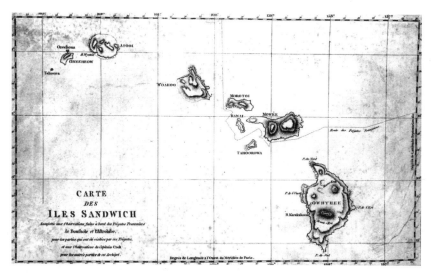

1798 French Map of the Sandwich Islands (Hawai'i Archives)

Between 1787 and 1790, an increasing number of English, American, French, Spanish, and Portuguese ships visited the three Island kingdoms. Trading was the main activity during this period. Foreigners were looked upon as partners in trade, which bolstered the chiefs' aspirations of glory.

> *To the natives it was an era of wonder, delight, and incipient disease; to the chiefs it was an El Dorado of iron and destructive implements, and visions of conquest grew as iron, and powder, and guns accumulated in the princely storerooms. The blood of the first discoverer had so rudely dispelled the illusion of the "Haole's" [foreigner's] divinity that now the natives, not only not feared them as superior beings, but actually looked upon them as serviceable, though valuable, materials to promote their interests and to execute their commands.*[22]

Kamehameha benefited from historical circumstances. First, a very high ranking former Maui chief, Ka'iana, joined Kamehameha's ranks in January of 1789 with a large cache of weapons and ammunition acquired during "three years in China and other lands."[23] After a failed rebellion against the Maui King Kahekili, Ka'iana, sought refuge under Kā'eo, King of Kaua'i, who was Kahekili's brother. In 1787, Ka'iana left the Kingdom of Kaua'i and was one of the first chiefs to leave the islands on a foreign trading vessel, the *Nootka*, accompanying Captain Meares to Canton, China, and the northwest coast of America. On his way to Kaua'i the following year, he landed on the Island Kingdom of Hawai'i at the court of

High Chief Ka'iana (Hawai'i Archives)

Kamehameha because he had fallen into disfavor with Kā'eo. Ka'iana was favorably received by Kamehameha due to his high aristocratic status, his renowned bravery, and for his cache of weapons. Kamehameha had also detained two Englishmen, John Young and Isaac Davis, who were skilled in muskets and artillery.[24] Kamehameha "was anxious to secure foreigners to teach him to handle the muskets which it had been his first object to obtain."[25]

> *These two captive foreigners…finding their lives secure and themselves treated with deference and kindness, were soon reconciled to their lot, accepted service under Kamehameha, and contributed greatly by their valor and skill to the conquests that he won, and by their counsel and tact to the consolidation of those conquests.*[26]

Keawema'uhili and Kamehameha reconciled their differences and in the spring of 1790, Keawema'uhili "sent a substantial contingent of canoes and warriors to aid" Kamehameha in his invasion of the Maui kingdom, which included the islands of Maui, Lāna'i, Moloka'i, and the former Kingdom of O'ahu.[27] Kahekili held his court at Waikīkī on the island of O'ahu, while his son Kalanikūpule governed the islands of Maui, Lāna'i and Moloka'i. When Kamehameha's forces landed on Maui, they overwhelmed the Maui chiefs and the decisive battles, known as *Kepaniwai* [damning of the waters] and *Kaua'upali* [clawed off the cliff], were fought in the valley of 'Īao. Kalanikūpule and some of his men escaped to O'ahu after the battle. Kamehameha's army soon overran the islands of Lāna'i and Moloka'i and prepared to invade the island of O'ahu.

Angered by Keawema'uhili's support of Kamehameha's Maui campaign, Keōua invaded Hilo and killed Keawema'uhili in battle, bringing Hilo under his control.[28] Taking advantage of Kamehameha's absence, Keōua proceeded to invade the districts of Hāmākua and Kohala and destroy Kamehameha's lands. Word of Keōua's pillage soon reached Kamehameha while he was preparing to invade O'ahu from Molokai and he was forced to abandon his plan and return to Hawai'i to deal with his sole remaining archrival for control of Hawai'i island. The islands of Maui and Moloka'i were later reclaimed without incident by the combined forces of an avenging Kahekili and his brother Kā'eo, King of Kaua'i, while Kalanikūpule remained on O'ahu to govern in his father's absence. The two leeward Kings then prepared to launch an invasion against Kamehameha from Maui.

Before Kamehameha returned from his leeward campaign, he sent one of his chiefs to consult with a renowned *kilokilo* [seer] resident on the island of O'ahu "to find out by what means he could make himself master of the whole of Hawai'i island."[29] Kamehameha was advised to "build a large Heiau [temple] for his god at Puukohola, adjoining the old Heiau of Mailekini near Kawaihae, Hawaii; that done, he would be supreme over Hawaii without more loss of life."[30] Upon his return, two unsuccessful battles with Keōua resulted in a stalemate, and Kamehameha refocused his energy and labor into the building of the grand heiau. It was an enormous task that involved the physical labor of Kamehameha and his people. However, soon he had to deal with the invading force of the two leeward Kings departing from Maui.

Kahekili and Kāʻeo sailed from Maui with a large fleet of canoes and invaded the northern coast of Hawaiʻi.[31] Kamehameha organized his forces, a multitude of schooners and double hulled canoes fixed with cannons, and sailed for Waipiʻo Valley to fight the leeward invaders.[32] The opposition force also had cannons but was no match against Kamehameha's fleet. In the naval battle, "the two fleets came together not far from Hawaiʻi...the battle was long and sanguinary."[33] Kamehameha defeated the leeward force in the battle of *Kepūwahaʻulaʻula* [red-mouth gun], but Kahekili and Kāʻeo and a few of their men managed to escape to their island kingdoms.

Refocusing his attention on the prophecy, Kamehameha returned to the task of constructing the great temple Puʻukoholā. In the summer of 1791, the grand heiau was completed and consecrated with full religious rites. Kamehameha's vision was to consolidate his dominion over the fractured Hawaiʻi island kingdom. He sent two of his chiefs, Keaweaheulu and Kamanawa, to meet with Keōua in Kaʻū. Keōua received Kamehameha's ambassadors with the customary formalities and agreed to accompany them to Puʻukoholā "to meet Kamehameha face to face and to make peace with him."[34] When Keōua entered the bay at Puʻukoholā by canoe, his party came under attack by Keʻeaumoku, one of Kamehameha's trusted advisers. Keōua was killed before he could set foot on the shoreline of the great temple. Whether by chance or design, the death of Keōua in 1791 was the final step of consolidating Kamehameha's rule over Hawaiʻi Island, reuniting the fractured Island Kingdom after nine years of civil war.

Puʻukoholā Heiau

Kamehameha "devoted the next few years to peace, the organization and administration of his government, and the normal development of the resources of his territory."[35] Kamehameha's grand design of conquering the leeward kingdoms was delayed at the request of Kahekili. While Kamehameha was on the island of Molokaʻi a year earlier, he sent an envoy to Kahekili's court at Waikīkī to arrange the place of battle. After consideration of the various plans, Kahekili replied:

Go, tell Kamehameha to return to Hawaiʻi, and when he learns that the black kapa covers the body of Kahekili and the sacrificial rites have been performed at his funeral, then Hawai'i shall be the Maika-stone that will sweep the course from here to Tahiti; let him then come and possess the country.[36]

FROM CHIEFLY TO BRITISH GOVERNANCE

Captain George Vancouver, commander of three English vessels, the *Discovery*, the *Chatham*, and the *Daedalus*, visited the islands on three separate occasions—March 1792, February-March 1793, and January-March 1794. The British Admiralty ordered Vancouver to complete the exploration of the northwest coast of the American continent initiated by the late Captain James Cook. In 1778, Cook named the island group the Sandwich Islands in honor of the First Lord of the British Admiralty, John Montagu, 4th Earl of Sandwich. Captain Vancouver was on good terms with all three kingdoms and even attempted to broker peace between them. Kamehameha and Captain Vancouver, however, became close friends and a bond developed between the Hawai'i King and the British. Kamehameha was aware of the tenuous relations with the leeward kingdoms, especially in the aftermath of the battle of *Kepūwaha'ula'ula*, and that another invasion would be attempted.

Captain George Vancouver

Kamehameha ceded the Island Kingdom of Hawai'i to Great Britain on February 25, 1794 and recognized King George III as emperor to ensure protection for the kingdom from both the leeward kings and foreign nations. The cession was a conditional mutual agreement recorded in the ship's log. The meeting took place on the British ship *Discovery*, with Kamehameha, his brothers Keli'imaika'i, and Kalaimamahū, chief of Hāmākua; Ke'eaumoku, chief of Kona; Keaweaheulu, chief of Ka'ū; Ka'iana, chief of Puna; Kame'eiamoku, chief of Kohala; and Kālaiwohi, half-brother of Kamehameha.[37]

The agreement provided that the British government would not interfere with the kingdom's religion, government and economy—"the chiefs and priests, were to continue as usual to officiate with the same authority as before in their respective stations."[38] Kamehameha and his Chiefs acknowledged they were part of the British Empire and subjects of King George III. Knowing that the religion would eventually have to conform to British custom, Kamehameha also "requested of Vancouver that on his return to England he would procure religious instructors to be sent to them from the country of which they now considered themselves subjects."[39] After the ceremony, the British ships fired a salute and delivered a copper plaque, which was placed at Kamehameha's residence. It read:

On the 25ᵗʰ of February, 1794, Tamaahmaah [Kamehameha], king of Owhyhee [Hawaiʻi], in council with the principal chiefs of the island assembled on board His Britannic Majesty's sloop Discovery in Karakakooa [Kealakekua] bay, and in the presence of George Vancouver, commander of the said sloop; Lieutenant Peter Puget, commander of his said Majesty's armed tender the Chatham; and the other officers of the Discovery; after due consideration, unanimously ceded the said island of Owhyhee [Hawaiʻi] to His Britannic Majesty, and acknowledged themselves to be subjects of Great Britain.[40]

Vancouver's fleet returned to Great Britain on March 3, 1794, and peace between the kingdoms lasted until the death of Kahekili in July 1794, when war broke out between the kingdoms of Maui and Kauaʻi. After the death of Kahekili, his son, Kalanikūpule, was recognized as the Mōʻī [King] of Maui, Lānaʻi, Molokaʻi, and Oʻahu.[41] While Kāʻeo, King of Kauaʻi and brother to Kahekili, would govern Maui and the adjacent islands, Kalanikūpule governed and held court at Waikīkī, island of Oʻahu. The arrangement of a shared kingdom caused tension between the Kauaʻi and Maui chiefs, and resulted in a battle. While Kāʻeo and his army prepared to depart from the leeward side of Oʻahu to his Kingdom of Kauaʻi, his chiefs planned to overthrow Kalanikūpule and bring the entire leeward islands under Kauaʻi rule. The Kauaʻi chiefs, assuming their King would not have supported the overthrow of his nephew, conspired to kill Kāʻeo by throwing him overboard while the fleet was deep in the channel between the islands of Oʻahu and Kauaʻi.[42]

Kāʻeo uncovered the plot, but instead of rounding up and seizing the conspirators, the Kauaʻi king decided to plan the invasion himself. The two armies met on the plains of Honolulu just above Pearl Harbor. With the assistance of two British trading ships, the *Jackall* and the *Prince Lee Boo* commanded by Captain Brown, Kalanikūpule defeated the invaders and Kāʻeo was killed on December of 1794.[43] The Kauaʻi chiefs abandoned the island of Oʻahu, and the Kingdom of Kauaʻi passed to Kaumualiʻi, son of the late king. After the battle, Kalanikūpule and his chiefs returned their attention to avenging their defeat four years earlier at the hands of Kamehameha, and prepared for an invasion of Hawaiʻi Island. According to Ralph Kuykendall, a historian:

Success inflated the ambition of Kalanikūpule and his chiefs and they began to dream of conquering Kamehameha. They thought perhaps that possession of foreign ships would make them invincible...A cunning plot was formed and on the first day of January, 1795, the Jackall *and the* Prince Lee Boo *were captured, the two captains, Brown and Gordon, were killed, and the surviving members of the crews were made prisoners.*[44]

Kalanikūpule's invasion plans were thwarted when the surviving crew managed to retake control of the ships off Waikīkī on January 12, 1795, and immediately sailed for the Island Kingdom of Hawaiʻi. The ships, containing the leeward King's arms and ammunition, landed in Hawaiʻi. Before they departed for Canton, China, Kamehameha learned of the murders of the two British Captains and Kalanikūpule's plan to invade his island.[45] As a British sub-ject, Kamehameha had a duty to avenge the deaths of the two British captains, and saw an opportunity for a pre-emptive strike against the Kingdom of Maui whose alliance with the Kingdom of Kauaʻi was now severed.

In February of 1795, Kamehameha left Hawaiʻi with an army of 16,000 men and quickly conquered Maui, Lānaʻi and Molokaʻi. On Molokaʻi, Kamehameha prepared for the invasion of Oʻahu where the majority of Kalanikūpule's army remained.[46] The final planning did not include Kaʻiana, because he had fallen into disfavor with Kamehameha for reasons, Hawaiian historians speculate, that were attributed to Kaʻiana's intimacy with Kaʻahumanu, one of the wives of Kamehameha. Thus Kaʻiana had no alternative but to break ranks with the Hawaiʻi king and join forces with the Maui king on Oʻahu.

In April 1795, Kamehameha and his forces landed on Oʻahu, and "for a while the victory was hotly contested; but the superiority of Kamehameha's artillery, the number of his guns, and the better practice of soldiers, soon turned the day in his favour, and the defeat of the Oahu forces became an accelerated rout and a promiscuous slaughter."[47] This was known as the battle of *Nuʻuanu*. Kaʻiana was killed by artillery and Kalanikūpule temporarily escaped capture, but was later found by Kamehameha's forces and killed. With the defeat of the Maui kingdom, Kamehameha ruled Hawaiʻi, Maui, Lānaʻi, Molokaʻi and Oʻahu. In April 1810, the Sandwich Islands came under Kamehameha's complete control when Kaumualiʻi ceded the Kingdom of Kauaʻi and its dependent island of Niʻihau, and recognized Kamehameha as his liege and lord. Kaumualiʻi was permitted to govern Kauaʻi with his own chiefs, but paid an annual tribute to Kamehameha.

COMMUNIQUÉS OF KAMEHAMEHA TO KING GEORGE III

Months before Kauaʻi was ceded, Kamehameha sent a letter, dated March 3, 1810 to King George III, together with a feathered cloak as a royal gift. Captain Spence, Master of the ship Duke of Portland, delivered the letter and gift. Spence handwrote the letter and Kamehameha signed it as "TAMAAHMAAH, King of the Sandwich Islands":

> *Having had no good opportunity of writing to you since Capt. Vancouver left here has been the means of my Silence. Capt. Vancouver Informed me you would send me a small vessel am sorry to say I have not yet received one.*[48]

> *Am sorry to hear your being at War with so many powers and I so far off cannot assist you. Should any of the powers which you are at War with molest me I shall expect your protection, and beg you will order your Ships of War & Privateer not to Capture any vessel whilst laying at Anchor in our Harbours, as I would thank you to make ours a neutral port as I have not the means of defence.*

> *I am in particular need of some Bunting having no English Colours also some brass Guns to defend the Islands in case of Attack from your Enemies. I have built a few small vessels*

with an Intent to trade on the North West of America with Tarro [taro] root the produce of these Islands for fur skins but am told by the White men here I cannot send them to sea without a Register. In consequence of which beg you will send me a form of a Register & seal with my Name on it.[49]

In order for Kamehameha to begin trading kalo [taro] on the northwest coast of America, he had to register the ships under British nationality in accordance with admiralty law.[50] Eighteenth century admiralty law made the "owner answerable for the contracts of the master, and it is said they also make the ship liable to the same."[51] The seal with Kamehameha's name was intended to authenticate the registration of the ships as a commissioned officer of the British Crown. Under British law, "important posts in government are conferred by the Crown by delivery of the seals of office and surrendered by delivery up of the seals."[52] According to F.W. Maitland, an English historian, seals were not "mere ceremonial symbols like the crown and the scepter; they are real instruments of government. Without a great seal, England could not be governed."[53]

King Kamehameha I (Hawai'i Archives)

Without a seal Kamehameha would not be able to register the ship's nationality for trading purposes, and therefore would also be unable to qualify the merchant ships' rights and protection under admiralty or maritime law. Of particular interest is in the postscript of the letter, where Kamehameha explained his reason for the invasion of the Kingdom of Maui and the change in royal residence from Hawai'i to O'ahu as being "in consequence of [Kalanikūpule's men] having put to death Mr. Brown & Mr. Gordon, Masters, (of the Jackall & Prince Lee Boo, two of you[r] merchant ships.)"[54] It is clear that Kamehameha's invasion was to avenge the deaths of the two British masters.

A second communication by Kamehameha dated August 6, 1810 informed King George III of the recent consolidation of the entire Sandwich Island group, and reiterated his former request for a government seal:

Kamehameha, King of the Sandwich Islands, wishing to render every assistance to the ships of his most sacred Majesty's subjects who visit these seas, have sent a letter by Captain Spence, ship "Duke of Portland," to his Majesty, since which Timoree [Kaumuali'i], King of Atooi [Kaua'i], has delivered his island up, and we are now in possession of the whole of the Sandwich Islands. We, as subjects to his most sacred Majesty, wish to have a seal and arms sent from Britain, so as there may be no molestation to our ships or vessels in those seas, or any hindrance whatever.[55]

In 1811, the Prince of Wales, son of King George III, became Prince Regent and ruled the British Empire after his father had a relapse of insanity. Captain Spence arrived in England during the royal transition and was unable to deliver Kamehameha's letter to King George III. The letter and gift of Kamehameha were instead delivered to the Prince Regent. In a communication from London dated April 30, 1812, Secretary of State for Foreign Affairs, the Earl of Liverpool, notified Kamehameha of the change in government. The Secretary of State assured Kamehameha that the Prince Regent would "promote the Welfare of the Sandwich Islands, and that He will give positive Orders to the Commanders of His Ships to treat with proper respect, all Trading Vessels belonging to you, or to Your subjects."[56]

Prince of Wales

He also stated that the Prince Regent was "confident that the Complete Success which He has gained over His Enemies in every Quarter of the Globe, will have the Effect of securing [Kamehameha's] Dominions from any attack or Molestation on their part."[57] However, the letter did not address Kamehameha's request for a register form and seal, preventing the ability to trade with merchants on the northwest coast of the American continent. Instead, Kamehameha found that he did not need a seal and registration to trade the kingdom's lucrative and vast amounts of sandalwood with merchant ships coming to his homeports.[58] This expansion of trade in the islands "afforded a convenient base of operation," and by 1812 there was "at least one agent established in Honolulu to coordinate the operations of several ships and to handle the business in the islands."[59]

With the leeward islands under his rule, Kamehameha incorporated and modified aspects of English governance, including the establishment of the office of a Prime Minister, and governors over the former kingdoms of Hawai'i, Maui and O'ahu.[60] The governors served as viceroys over the lands of the former kingdoms "with legislative and other powers almost as extensive as those kings whose places they took."[61] *Kālaimoku* (carver of lands) was the ancient name given to a King's chief counselor, and became the native equivalent to a Prime Minister. Kamehameha appointed Kalanimōkū as his Prime Minister and he thereafter took on the name of his title—*Kālaimoku*. Foreigners also commonly referred to him as Billy Pitt, the namesake of the younger William Pitt who served as Britain's Prime Minister under King George III. Kālaimoku's duty was to manage day-to-day operations of the national government, as well as to be commander-in-chief of all the military, and head of the kingdom's treasury. Samuel Kamakau, a Hawaiian historian, explained:

> *By this appointment Kamehameha waived the privilege of giving anything away*
> *without the consent of the treasurer. Should that officer fail to confirm a gift it would not*
> *be binding. Kamehameha could not give any of the revenues of food or fish on his own*

account in the absence of this officer. If he were staying, not in Kailua but in Kawaihae or Hōnaunau, the treasurer had to be sent for, and only upon his arrival could things be given away to chiefs, lesser chiefs, soldiers, to the chief's men, or to any others. The laws determining life or death were in the hands of this treasurer; he had charge of everything. Kamehameha's brothers, the chiefs, the favorites, the lesser chiefs, the soldiers, and all who were fed by the chief, anyone to whom Kamehameha gave a gift, could secure it to himself only by informing the chief treasurer.[62]

Kamehameha established a national council comprised of the three governors, other high chiefs, and the King's trusted foreign advisors—John Young and Isaac Davis. In effect, Kamehameha established a federal system with two-levels of government. At the higher level, the national government had authority over the four former kingdoms and addressed matters of national interests and foreign policy, while at the lower level Kamehameha's vassals governed day-to-day matters among their tenants under a feudal tenure. National and regional authorities were independent except for their common allegiance to Kamehameha. A Prime Minister headed the national government, while sovereignty resided in the King. John Young and Isaac Davis advised Kamehameha on the establishment of this form of government. In 1794, Captain Vancouver made the following comments regarding the two men, who were influential in forming the government of the Sandwich Islands along English custom:

> *I likewise beg leave to recommend Messrs. John Young and Isaac Davis, to whose services not only the persons, &c., under my command have been highly indebted for their good offices, but am convinced that through the uniformity of their conduct and unremitting good advise to Tamaahmaah [Kamehameha] and the different chiefs, that they have been materially instrumental in causing the honest, civil and attentive behavior lately experienced by all visitors from the inhabitants of this island.*[63]

Chiefs of Kamehameha I (Hawai'i Archives)

As a feudal monarchy, the lands of the kingdom, with the exception of Kaua'i,[64] were divided between Kamehameha and his four principal chiefs, Keaweaheulu, Ke'eaumoku, Kame'eiamoku and Kamanawa. Each chief was each given "large tracts of lands from Hawai'i to O'ahu in payment for their services."[65] Kamehameha and the chiefs divided their lands with their lesser chiefs, until it reached the common tenant by subsequent divisions—each person in the chain bearing allegiance to their superior from the lowest class of tenants, through the levels of chiefs, to Kamehameha. In return for the lands, the chiefs owed military service when called upon, while the commoners owed labor and the produce of the soil and ocean.

Although each principal Chief was independent to govern his own newly acquired districts, the traditional ancient laws of the kingdoms were the equivalent of a written code.[66] Kamehameha "put an end to wars, erected a strong central government, checked the oppression of the lesser chiefs, appointed officers more for merit than rank, improved the laws, made them more uniform, rigidly enforced them, and generally brought about a condition of comparative peace and security."[67] Native religion organized and stratified the regional authorities, while British principles of governance at the national level organized and stratified the roles of the King, Prime Minister and governors.

CHAPTER 2
REIGN OF KAMEHAMEHA II

*I*n 1809, Kamehameha decreed his son Liholiho, styled Kamehameha II, heir to the throne, but according to his last will, Ka'ahumanu would serve as his Prime Minister, replacing Kalanimōkū. The use of the term Prime Minister would be replaced with Premier, and the native term *Kālaimoku* with *Kuhina Nui*, a term specifically translated as Premier. After Kamehameha died on May 8, 1819, Kamehameha II instituted a radical change by eliminating the religious laws, relying solely on chiefly laws for governance. The most prominent law was the *'ai kapu* (eating restriction). Accordingly, men and women ate separately, and women were forbidden to eat pork, bananas, coconuts, and particular types of fish, shark, turtle, porpoise and whale.[68] Any infraction of this *kapu* (taboo) was punishable by death.

King Kamehameha II (Hawai'i Archives)

Kamakau explained that, "free eating followed the death of the ruling chief," but "after the period of mourning was over the new ruler placed the land under a new tabu following old lines." According to Kamakau, the overthrow of the religion was warranted, and "in this case Kamehameha II merely continued the practice of free eating."[69] The repudiation of the eating kapu set in motion a chain of events that culminated in the order to destroy all religious temples and idols throughout the realm. The overthrow of the religion not only created a political vacuum to be filled with more chiefly edicts, but it also threw into question the organization and stratification of Hawaiian society that religion had dictated for centuries. The abolition of the religion, however, "allowed people more flexibility in their dealings with the increasing numbers of foreigners."[70]

INTRODUCTION OF CHRISTIANITY

When American missionaries arrived in the kingdom in March of 1820 the Hawaiian religion had been abolished, but these missionaries were not the "religious instructors whom the King and chiefs expected from England." When they realized that the missionaries were from the United States, they initially were prohibited from landing, but were finally allowed to come on shore only at the "assurance of the English settler, John Young (Olohana), that they came to preach the same religion as the English missionaries"[71] Kamehameha II granted the American missionaries a license of one-year residency which he later extended.

John Young (Olohana) (Hawai'i Archives)

For the next four years the missionaries developed a written form of the Hawaiian language, provided instruction on reading and writing, and taught the Christian religion. This teaching was initially limited to the chiefly class. If the missionaries "could not win the Chiefs they had little chance of success with the common people."[72] The abolition of the Hawaiian religion reinforced the consolidation of authority in the chiefly class and caused much oppression.[73] The chiefs would decide whether or not the missionaries would have access to the common people.

On November 27, 1823, Kamehameha II went on a diplomatic mission to England and the kingdom came under the administration of Ka'ahumanu as Regent and Kalanimōkū as Premier. The King's mission was to confirm the cession of his father's kingdom to Great Britain in 1794, which later included the former kingdoms of Maui and Kaua'i. After Kamehameha II's departure, Ka'ahumanu formally declared Christianity the new religion of the country on December 21, 1823, requiring strict observance of the Sabbath.[74] Six months later she proclaimed, by crier laws, prohibition of murder, theft of any description, boxing or fighting among the people, and added that "when schools are established, all the people shall learn the *palapala* [reading and writing]."[75] On April 13, 1824, Ka'ahumanu met with the chiefs in council in Honolulu "to make known their decision to extend the teaching of *palapala* and the word of God to the common people."[76]

These events not only paved the way for universal literacy, but also filled the void left in 1819 by the abolition of the Hawaiian religion and replaced it with Christianity. The missionaries adopted a role similar to that held by the priests under the old religion, where "it was the duty of the high priest to urge the king most strenuously to direct his thoughts to the gods; to worship them without swerving; [and] to be always obedient to their commands with absolute sincerity and devotedness."[77] Consequently, the use of Jehovah in the chiefly laws was reminiscent of the use of the deities of Kū, Kāne, Lono and Kanaloa in Kamehameha's time. As the old religion organized and stratified Hawaiian society, the Christian religion would do the same, serving as the unwritten constitution of the country. Mosaic law, in theory, became the foundational or organic law for the chiefs and commoners, which was supplemented by native customary law and edicts of the chiefs.

Under this new federal system of governance, the four principal chiefs and their successor children were the regional administrators over the lands given to them by Kamehameha. The laws were not uniformly enforced throughout the islands, except for the laws proclaimed by the King or Regent at the national level. Compounding the problem was the duplicity of governance—regional governance for the native population, and national governance for the foreign population. Governance over foreigners was extremely problematic because foreigners did not view themselves as subject to the King, but rather as subject to the laws of their native countries. It soon became apparent that this system could not address the increased presence and demands of the foreign population. Consequently, a move toward a single level government and adherence to "common law" principles over the entire country became not only necessary as a practical matter, but also for the survival of the Kingdom.

SANDWICH ISLAND DELEGATION MEETS WITH KING GEORGE IV

Before Kamehameha II could meet with King George IV, he and his Queen, Kamāmalu, contracted measles in London. Kamāmalu died on July 8, 1824, followed by the King six days later. In the month before Kamehameha II died, he wrote a letter to Kalanimōkū, Ka'ahumanu, and his younger brother, Kauikeaouli.[78] He explained that when the delegation arrived in London, a representative of King George IV told them "he was to see to all of [their] needs and...will pay all expenses," and that the "King of England has taken a great liking to us."[79] After asserting that his delegation had not yet met the King, he reported that he, his wife and one of the chiefs, Kapihe, were ill. But his letter concluded that "we will remain until we see the King," for "when we obtain that which will be of great benefit to us, then we will return."[80] The benefit he alluded to was the assurance of British protection from foreign powers, which was the subject of a letter he sent to King George IV on August 21, 1822 before departing for London:

> I avail myself of this opportunity of acquainting your Majesty of the death of my father, Kamehameha, who departed this life the 8th of May, 1819, much lamented by his subjects; and, having appointed me his successor, I have enjoyed a happy reign ever since that period; and I assure your Majesty it is my sincere wish to be thought as worthy of your attention as my father had the happiness to be, during the visit of Captain Vancouver. The whole of these islands having been conquered by my father, I have succeeded to the government of them, and beg leave to place them all under the protection of your most excellent Majesty; wishing to observe peace with all nations, and to be thought worthy the confidence I place in your Majesty's wisdom and judgement.

The former idolatrous system has been abolished in these islands, as we wish the Protestant religion of your Majesty's dominions to be practiced here. I hope your Majesty may deem it fit to answer this as soon as convenient; and your Majesty's counsel and advice will be most thankfully received by your Majesty's most obedient and devoted servant.[81]

High Chief and Chiefess Boki and Liliha (Hawai'i Archives)

On September 11, 1824, the Sandwich Island delegation, (headed by Boki, the group's ranking chief and brother to Kalanimoku), met with King George IV. Accompanying Boki was his wife, Liliha, and the four remaining chiefs of the delegation—Kapihe, Naukana, Kekūanao'a, and James Young Kānehoa. The King's Prime Minister, Robert Jenkinson, and the Foreign Secretary, George Canning, also attended. Boki explained to the British king that the Sandwich Island delegation wished to "confirm the words which Kamehameha I gave in charge to Vancouver" in 1794, and by that agreement Kamehameha acknowledged King George III as his "superior."[82] In response, King George IV reiterated the position in his communication with Kamehameha as Prince Regent in 1812: that the Sandwich Islands were considered a British protectorate.[83] Kekūanao'a recalled King George IV's statement:

I have heard these words, I will attend to the evils from without. The evils within your Kingdom it is not for me to regard; they are with yourselves. Return and say to the King, to Ka'ahumanu and to Kālaimoku, I will watch over it, lest evils should come from others to the Kingdom. I therefore will watch over him agreeably to those ancient words.[84]

King George IV appointed Richard Charlton as British consul to both the Kingdom of the Sandwich Islands and the Society Islands, and Charlton arrived with his wife in Honolulu on April 16, 1825.

CHAPTER 3
ASSERTING HAWAIIAN SOVEREIGNTY

On May 4th 1825, *HBMS Blonde*, under the command of Lord George Anson Bryon, arrived at Lahaina with the bodies of Kamehameha II and Kamāmalu. Lord Byron held, in his possession, secret instructions from the British Crown regarding the native government of the Sandwich Islands and specific actions to be taken with foreign powers if they exerted sovereignty over the islands. Lord Byron informed British Consul Charlton of these secret instructions. The following is reprinted in its entirety to grasp the full scope of Britain's view of the Sandwich Islands, which specifically adheres to the conditions of the 1794 cession entered into by agreement between Vancouver and Kamehameha whereby "the chiefs and priests, were to continue as usual to officiate with the same authority as before in their respective stations."[85]

[Open with the announcement of Mr. Charlton's being authorized to look after and protect British subjects in the Friendly, Society, and Sandwich Islands. Orders to Lord Byron to land the bodies of the King and Queen,] with such marks of respect as may be proper and acceptable to the Natives, you proceed to make yourself acquainted with the existing government, and the internal state of this group of Islands, as well as with the influence and interests which any foreign Powers may have in them.

If any Disputes as to the Succession on the Death of the late King should unhappily arise, you will endeavour to maintain a strict Neutrality, and if forced to take any Part, you will espouse that which you shall find to be most consistent with established Laws and Customs of that People.

You will endeavor to cultivate a good Understanding with the Government, in whatever native Hands it may be, and to secure, by kind Offices and friendly Intercourse, a future and lasting Protection for the Persons and Property of the Subjects of the United Kingdom.

As my Lords have directed that you should be furnished with the voyages of Captains Cooke and Vancouver, and that of Captain Kotzebue of the Russian Navy, and an essay on the commerce of the Pacific by Captain Macconochie, you will be apprized of the position in which these Islands stand with regard to the Crown of Great Britain, and that His Majesty might claim over them a right of sovereignty not only by discovery, but by a direct and formal Cession by the Natives, and by the virtual acknowledgement of the Officers of Foreign Powers.

The right of His Majesty does not think it necessary to advance directly in opposition to, or in controul of, any native Authority:—with such the question should not be raised, and, if proposed, had better be evaded, in order to avoid any differences or Sentiment on an occasion so peculiar as your present Mission to those Islands; but if any Foreign Power or its Agents should attempt, or have attempted, to establish any Sovereignty or possession (of which a remarkable instance is mentioned, with disapprobation, by Captain Kotzbue), you are then to assert the prior rights of His Majesty, but in such a manner as may leave untouched the actual relations between His Majesty and the Government of the Sandwich Islands; and if by circumstances you should be obliged to come to a specific declaration, you are to take the Islands under His Majesty's protection, and to deny the right of any other Power to assume any Sovereignty, or to make any exclusive settlement in any of that group.

In all matters of this nature, so much must depend on the actual state of affairs, which at this distance of time and place cannot be foreseen, that my Lords can give you no more particular instructions; but their Lordships confide in your Judgment and Discretion in treating unforeseen Circumstances according to the Principles of Justice and Humanity which actuate H[is] M[ajesty]'s Councils, and They recommend to You, that while You are ready to assert and vindicate H[is] M[ajesty]'s Rights, you will pay the greatest Regard to the Comfort, the Feelings, and even the Prejudices of the Natives, and will show the utmost Moderation towards the Subjects of any other Powers, whom you may meet in those Islands.

H[is] M[ajesty]'s Rights you will, if necessary, be prepared to assert, but considering the Distance of the Place, and the Infant State of political Society there, You will avoid, as far as may be possible, the bringing these Rights into Discussion, and will propose that any disputed Point between Yourself and any Subjects of other Powers shall be referred to your respective Governments.[86]

After the funeral and time of mourning had passed, the Council of Chiefs met on June 6, 1824, in Honolulu with Lord Byron and the British Consul. It was confirmed that Liholiho's brother, Kauikeaouli, was to be Kamehameha III, but since he was only eleven years old, Ka'ahumanu would continue to serve as Regent and Kalanimōkū as Premier. Kalanimōkū addressed the Council "setting forth the defects of many of their laws and customs, particularly the reversion of lands" to a new King for redistribution and assignment.[87] The chiefs collectively agreed to forgo this ancient custom, and the lands were maintained in the hands of the original *tenants in chief* and their successors, subject to reversion only in times of treason.[88] Lord Byron was invited to address the Council, and without violating his specific orders of non-intervention

Kalanimoku (Hawai'i Archives)

in the political affairs of the kingdom, he prepared eight recommendations on paper and presented it to the chiefs for their consideration.

1. That the king be head of the people.
2. That all the chiefs swear allegiance.
3. That the lands descend in hereditary succession.
4. That taxes be established to support the king.
5. That no man's life be taken except by consent of the king or regent and twelve chiefs.
6. That the king or regent grant pardons at all times.
7. That all the people be free and not bound to one chief.
8. That a port duty be laid on all foreign vessels.[89]

King Kamehameha III
(Hawai'i Archives)

Lord Byron introduced the fundamental principles of British governance to the chiefs and set them on a course of national consolidation and uniformity. His suggestions referred "to the form of government, and the respective and relative rights of the king, chiefs, and people, and to the tenure of lands,"[90] but not to a uniform code of laws. Since the death of Kamehameha in 1819, the Hawaiian Kingdom, as a feudal autocracy, had no uniform system of laws systematically applied throughout the islands. Rather it fell on each of the *tenants in chief* and their designated vassals to be both lawmaker and arbiter over their own particular tenants living on the granted lands from the King.

It is not clear whether Ka'ahumanu and the Council of Chiefs clearly understood their relationship with Great Britain as a protectorate, but it was evident that the lines of communication between Great Britain and the Sandwich Islands, through its resident Consul Charlton, had become strained. This could account for the action taken by Ka'ahumanu and the Council of Chiefs when they entered into a treaty with Captain Thomas Catesby Jones, on behalf of the United States.

> *On the 22d of December, 1826, a great council of chiefs was convoked by the queen regent, at which Captain Jones and the British consul were present. At this council Mr. Charlton declared that the islanders were subjects of Great Britain, and denied their right to make treaties, to which Captain Jones replied that Charlton's own commission as consul recognized the independence of the islands. The council then proceeded to business, and soon agreed to the terms of the commercial treaty with the United States, the first between the Hawaiian Government and any foreign power.*[91]

With this treaty, Ka'ahumanu, the Council of Chiefs, and the United States, directly challenged British sovereignty over the Sandwich Islands. Article two read, "The ships and vessels of the United States, (as well as their Consuls and all other citizens,) within the territorial jurisdiction of the Sandwich Islands, together with all their property, shall be inviolably protected against all enemies of the United States in time of war."[92]   An apparent conflict would arise if Great Britain, as the protector State, became an enemy of the United States as it was during the War of 1812. Despite the failure of the United States Senate to ratify the treaty, Kaʻahumanu and the Council of Chiefs adhered to its terms in its relations with United States ships and citizens.

CODE OF LAWS

Kaʻahumanu called a meeting of the Council of Chiefs on December 7, 1827, to address "the act of Kamehameha in giving up the islands to the protection of Great Britain,"[93] and to discuss the authority of drafting a national code of laws for the kingdom. The chiefs were still unclear as to the meaning of the words spoken by King George IV to the Sandwich Island delegation in 1824, and whether they might draft a code of laws on their own or would need British approval. Kaʻahumanu and the Council of Chiefs were not aware of the secret instructions given to Lord Byron asserting that the Sandwich Islands were British. After an emphatic debate on the topic, Kaʻahumanu accused Richard Charlton, the British consul, of being "a liar and that no confidence is to be placed in anything that he says."[94]   The chiefs understood the British relationship to be that of comity rather than vassalage, therefore they were "fully convinced that it would not do to send to England for laws; but that they must make them themselves."[95]

The first national code of laws was a penal code of three laws enacted by Kamehameha III with the advice and consent of the Council of Chiefs prohibiting murder, theft and adultery. Murder was punishable by death, and theft and adultery were punishable by imprisonment in irons. Three additional laws prohibiting the selling of rum, prostitution, and gambling were later added to the code, and proclaimed together as the first penal laws of the kingdom on December 8, 1827. The enforcement of these penal laws resided within the multi-leveled feudal structure of various mesne *chiefs* who ruled over the people. The "rule of law" had not yet been laid as the cornerstone of constitutional governance and enforcement of the law was not uniform, but it was a move towards a unified governance.

By 1829, Kamehameha III, only fifteen years old, took an active role in the affairs of government,[96] and together with Kaʻahumanu, as Premier, and the Council, asserted that the kingdom was not a British dependency, but a separate and autonomous nation. Captain William Finch of the *USS Vincennes*, visiting the island group in 1829, heard for the first time the use of the word *Hawaiian*, and took notice of a deliberate movement by the government of the islands to form a distinct national identity.

> *The Government and Natives generally have dropped or do not admit the designation of Sandwich Islands as applied to their possessions; but adopt and use that of Hawaiian; in allusion to the fact of the whole Groupe having been subjugated by the first Tamehameha [Kamehameha], who was the Chief of the principal Island of Owhyhee, or more modernly Hawaii.*[97]

Upon the death of Ka'ahumanu in 1832, Kamehameha III assumed full control of government and appointed Kīna'u as the Premier. In 1834, a more expansive penal code was enacted with five chapters, and "each chapter was discussed and ratified by the council of chiefs according to ancient custom before receiving the King's signature and becoming law."[98]

Ka'ahumanu with Attendant (Hawai'i Archives)

FACING RELIGIOUS TOLERANCE

Religious tolerance did not enter the political scene until 1827 when a Catholic missionary party arrived in Honolulu on July 7th onboard the ship *Comete* from the French port city of Bordeaux.[99] Unlike the American Protestants who received a conditional license from Kamehameha II in 1820, the Catholic missionary party made no request for a license to stay, yet for the next two years they were able to establish a small following of the native population. By order of Ka'ahumanu on January 3, 1830, the teaching of the Catholic religion was forbidden throughout the kingdom, and the Catholic priests, one of whom was a British subject, were expelled from the country on December 24, 1831.[100]

In Hawai'i, religion was as much a part of chiefly governance as governance was an extension of religion. While religion constituted the organic laws of the country, administratively; governance resided solely with the King and his chiefs. The only change that took place was the *form* of religion—from the strict religious kapu to Christianity, although the chiefs still governed in principle. Catholicism represented not only a challenge to the Protestant faith, but also a direct challenge to the authority of the chiefs. Native Catholics were routinely subjected to persecution and punishment at the hands of the chiefs.

On September 30th 1836, another British Catholic priest, arrived by direction of the Order of the Sacred Hearts, and the government's anti-Catholic policy was again the subject of dispute by foreigners. This prompted Kamehameha III to issue the following ordinance on December 18, 1837:

1837 Ordinance Rejecting the Catholic Religion (Hawai'i Archives)

As we have seen the peculiarities of the Catholic religion and the proceedings of the priests of the Roman faith, to be calculated to set man against man in our kingdom, and as we formerly saw the disturbance was made in the time of Ka'ahumanu I. and as it was on this account that the priests of the Romish faith were at that time banished and sent away from this kingdom, and as from that time they have been under sentence of banishment until within this past year when we have been brought into new and increased trouble on account of the request of foreigners that we make it known in writing. Therefore, I, with my chiefs, forbid…that anyone should teach the peculiarities of the Pope's religion nor shall it be allowed to anyone who teaches those doctrines of those peculiarities to reside in this kingdom; nor shall the ceremonies be permitted to land on these shores; for it is not proper that two religions be found in this small kingdom. Therefore we utterly refuse to allow anyone to teach those peculiarities in any manner whatsoever. We moreover prohibit all vessels whatsoever from bringing any teacher of that religion into this kingdom.[101]

As per the ordinance, followers of the Catholic religion were persecuted and imprisoned. However, about a year and a half later, there was a change. On June 17, 1839, Kamehameha III issued "orders that no more punishments should be inflicted; and that all who were then in confinement, should be released" and all of the native prisoners were freed from the Honolulu Fort.[102] A French warship was dispatched to the islands under the command of Captain Cyrille Laplace in response to the reported claims of unfair treatment of Catholics and arrived at Honolulu on July 9, 1839. When the French warship arrived, Laplace informed Kamehameha III, "the formal intention of France that the king of the Sandwich Islands be powerful, independent of foreign power, and that he consider her his ally; but she also demands that he conform to the usages of civilized nations."[103] Captain Laplace issued the following five demands:

1. That the Catholic worship be declared free throughout all the islands subject to the king.
2. That a site at Honolulu for a Catholic church be given by the government.
3. That all Catholics imprisoned on account of their religion be immediately set at liberty.
4. That the king place in the hands of the captain of the "Artemise" the sum of twenty thousand dollars as a guarantee of his future conduct toward France; to be restored when it shall be considered that the accompanying treaty will be faithfully complied with.
5. That the treaty, signed by the king, as well as the money, be brought on board of the frigate "Artemise" by a principal chief; and that the French flag be saluted with twenty-one guns.

These are the equitable conditions at the price of which the king of the Sandwich Islands shall preserve friendship with France...If contrary to expectation, and misled by bad advisers, the king and chiefs refuse to sign the treaty I present, war will immediately commence, and all the devastations and calamities which may result shall be imputed to them alone, and they must also pay damages which foreigners injured under these circumstances will have a right to claim.[104]

Before Captain Laplace could carry out the threat of hostilities, the Premier, Miriam Kekāuluohi, and the Governor of Oʻahu, Kekūanaoʻa, were forced to sign the French treaty on behalf of Kamehameha III who was still en route to Honolulu from the kingdom's capital city of La-haina, Maui. The Hawaiian government managed to borrow $20,000 from foreign merchants in Honolulu. The funds filled four boxes and were sealed by the government's wax seal. On the morning of June 14, 1839, Kamehameha III arrived in Honolulu, and Captain Laplace, not feeling satisfied, compelled the King to sign an additional convention of eight articles on June 16th that imposed jury selection benefits to Frenchmen and a fixed duty on French wine or brandy not to exceed five percent *ad valorem*. Undeterred by foreign aggression, Kamehameha III and his chiefs pursued government reform that sought to establish as well as protect the rights of its people.

KEY CONCEPTS

Religious Law   Chiefly law   Cession
Federal system   Prime Minister   Religious Tolerance

FURTHER CONSIDERATION

1. Most people believe that Kamehameha was merely on friendly terms with the British. However, the cession of the Kingdom of Hawai'i Island on February 24, 1794, and the letters of Kamehameha to King George III in 1810 clearly show that the Kingdom of the Sandwich Islands was British. Why do you think people were taught otherwise?

2. A year before the American missionaries arrived in the Sandwich Islands the ancient religion was abolished. What do you think were the circumstances that led to this event, and could it be that the abolishing of the religion was predetermined if Kamehameha requested Captain Vancouver to send over British missionaries in 1794?

3. Write a script or role-play (with others) a meeting of the National Council of Chiefs where Ka'ahumanu announced the prohibition of teaching the Catholic religion in the kingdom. What was her reasoning for such a decree and how could she have justified it before the Council? From her perspective what was the difference between Protestantism and Catholicism since both derived from the Christian faith?

[1] Kāʻeo was also the brother of Kahekili, the Maui King.

[2] In a manner resembling that of King Egbert of Wessex and his consolidation in 829 A.D. of the seven Anglo-Saxon kingdoms of southeast Britain that later came to be known as England. F.M. Stenton, *Anglo-Saxon England* (Clarendon Press 1943), 230.

[3] Eli Sagan, *At the Dawn of Tyranny: The Origins of Individualism, Political Oppression, and the State* (Alfred A. Knopf 1985), xxi.

[4] W.D. Alexander, "A Brief History of Land Titles in the Hawaiian Kingdom," *Interior Department, Appendix to Surveyor General's Report to the 1882 Hawaiian Legislature*, 3.

[5] "The Hawaiian Flag," *Hawaiian Almanac and Annual* (Thos. G. Thrum 1880), 24.

[6] Secretary of State J.C. Calhoun sent a letter stating the United States recognized Hawaiʻi's sovereignty.

[7] David Malo, *Hawaiian Antiquities* (Bishop Museum 1951), 187.

[8] *Id.*, 191.

[9] Sheldon Dibble, *A History of the Sandwich Islands* (Thomas G. Thrum, Publisher 1909), 72.

[10] Samuel Mānaiakalani Kamakau, *Ka Poʻe Kahiko: The People of Old* (The Bishop Museum Press 1964), 11

[11] Malo, 53.

[12] Walter Frear, "The Evolution of the Hawaiian Judiciary," *Papers of the Hawaiian Historical Society* (June 29, 1894), 1.

[13] Abraham Fornander, *Ancient History of the Hawaiian People to the Times of Kamehameha I* (Mutual Publishing 1996), 204.

[14] *Id.*, 303.

[15] *Id.*, 302.

[16] Samuel M. Kamakau, *Ruling Chiefs of Hawaiʻi* (Kamehameha Schools Press 1992), 120.

[17] Fornander, 308.

[18] Kamakau, *Ruling Chiefs*, 121.

[19] Fornander, 311.

[20] *Id.*, 320.

[21] *Id.*

[22] *Id.*

[23] Kamakau, *Ruling Chiefs*, 144.

[24] Thomas Thrum, "John Young: Companion of Kamehameha, a Brief Sketch of His Life in Hawaiʻi," *Hawaiian Almanac and Annual* (Thos. G. Thrum 1910), 96. During Captain Vancouver's second trip to the islands in 1793 he identifies John Young to be "about forty-four years of age, born at Liverpool, and Isaac Davis, then thirty-six years old, born at Milford."

[25] *Id.*, 146.

[26] Fornander, 235.

[27] Ralph S. Kuykendall, *The Hawaiian Kingdom: 1778-1854, Foundation and Transformation*, vol. 1 (University of Hawaiʻi Press 1938), 35.

[28] Kamakau, *Ruling Chiefs*, 151.

[29] Kuykendall, 36.

[30] Fornander, 240.

[31] Kuykendall, 37.

[32] Kamakau, *Ruling Chiefs*, 161.

[33] Kuykendall, 37.

[34] *Id.*, 37.

[35] *Id.*, 38.

[36] Fornander, 239.

[37] Id., 342.

[38] George Vancouver, *Voyage of Discovery to the North Pacific Ocean and the round the World*, vol. 3 (Da Capo Press 1967), 56.

[39] Manly Hopkins, Hawaii: *The Past, Present and Future of Its Island Kingdom* (Kegan Paul 2003), 133.

[40] *Id.*

[41] Fornander, 262.

[42] *Id.*, 263.

[43] *Id.*, 343.

[44] Kuykendall, 46.

[45] Fornander, 343.

[46] *Id.*, 347.

[47] Fornander, 348.

[48] James Jackson Jarves, *History of the Hawaiian Islands*, 3rd ed. (Charles Edwin Hitchcock 1847), 117. This schooner was finally delivered to Kamehameha's successor on May 1, 1822, by Captain Kent on behalf of King George IV. The name of the schooner was the Prince Regent.

[49] Rhoda E.A. Hackler, "Alliance or Cession? Missing Letter from Kamehameha I to King George III of England Casts Light on 1794 Agreement," *The Hawaiian Journal of History* 20 (1986): 1-12, 7.

[50] Arthur Brown, *A Compendious View of the Civil Law, and of the Law of the Admiralty*, 2nd ed. (G. Woodfall 1802), 75.

[51] *Id*, 35.

[52] David M. Walker, *The Oxford Companion to Law* (Clarendon Press 1980), 1122.

[53] F.W. Maitland, *The Constitutional History of England* (University Press 1926), 393.

[54] Hackler, 56.

[55] Hopkins, 131.

[56] *Liverpool to Kamehameha*, April 30, 1812, Hawai'i Archives, F.O.E.X., Series 402 Box 2.

[57] *Id.*

[58] Kuykendall, 84-89.

[59] *Id.*, 85.

[60] Walter Frear, "Hawaiian Statute Law," *Thirteenth Annual Report of the Hawaiian Historical Society* (Hawaiian Gazette Co., Ltd. 1906). Frear mistakenly states Kamehameha established four earldoms that included the Kingdom of Kaua'i. Kaumuali'i was not a governor, but remained a King. A governor was not established until July 1821 after Kamehameha II removed Kaumuali'i to O'ahu and appointed Ke'eaumoku, the junior of one of Kamehameha I's Kona Chiefs, as governor of Kaua'i.

[61] *Id.*

[62] Kamakau, *Ruling Chiefs*, 175.

[63] Thrum, 99.

[64] On 8 August 1824, the Kaua'i chiefs unsuccessfully rebelled under Humehume, son of Kaumuali'i, King of Kaua'i. Humehume was removed to O'ahu under the watch of Kalanimoku, and all of the Kaua'i chiefs were dispersed throughout the other islands and their lands replaced with Hawai'i island chiefs.

[65] Kamakau, *Ruling Chiefs*, 175.

[66] Jarves, 86.

[67] Frear, 19.

[68] Malo, 29.

[69] *Id.*, 222.

[70] Juri Mykkanen, *Inventing Politics: A New Political Anthropology of the Hawaiian Kingdom*, (University of Hawai'i Press 2003), 35.

[71] Hopkins, 133.

[72] *Id.*, 104.

[73] *Id.*

[74] Kuykendall, 117.

[75] *Id.*, 118.

[76] Mykkanen, 49.

[77] Malo, 188.

[78] Kamehameha II's letter was addressed to Pa'alua, Ka'akumu and his younger brother. Pa'alua was another name for Kalanimoku and there is no record of a chief or chiefess named Ka'akumu. It may be a misspelling of Ka'ahumanu instead.

[79] *King Kamehameha II letter from London*, (translation), F.O. & Ex, Hawai'i Archives.

[80] *Id.*

[81] Jarves, 118.

[82] "Reverend William Richards Record of Kekūanao'a's Testimony of What Was Said at the Court of Saint James, 1824," Archives of Hawai'i; also printed in the Polynesian Newspaper, October 18, 1851. In his recounting of what took place Kekūanao'a mistakenly referred to Mr. Canning as the Kālaimoku, a native term synonymous with Prime Minister.

[83] *Liverpool to Kamehameha*.

[84] Richards Record of Kekūanao'a's Testimony.

[85] Vancouver, 56.

[86] Secret Instructions to Lord Byron, September 14, 1824, BPRO, Adm. 2/1693, pages 241-245, printed in Report of the Historical Commission of the Territory of Hawai'i for the two years ending December 31, 1926, 19.

[87] Jarves, 122.

[88] *Id.*

[89] Voyage of H.M.S. Blonde, 155; reprinted in Kuydendall, 120.

[90] C.S. Stewart, *A Visit to the South Seas, in the U.S. Ship Vincennes, during the years 1829 and 1830*, (New York: Sleight & Robinson, 1831), 148.

[91] W.D. Alexander, *A Brief History of the Hawaiian People* (American Book Company 1891), 197.

[92] *Treaties and Conventions Concluded between the Hawaiian Kingdom and other Powers, since 1825* (Elele Book, Card and Job Print 1887), 1.

[93] Chamberlain Journal, November 3, 1827.

[94] Chamberlain to Whitney and Ruggles, Dec. 17-27, MS in HMCS Library.

[95] *Id.*

[96] Jarves, 134.

[97] "Capt. Finch's Cruise in the U.S.S. Vincennes," U.S. Navy Department Archives.

[98] W.D. Westervelt, "Hawaiian Printed Laws Before the Constitution," *Sixteenth Annual Report of the Hawaiian Historical Society and Papers, December 31, 1908* (Hawaiian Gazette Co., Ltd. 1909), 48.

[99] Kuykendall, 139.

[100] *Id.*, 142.

[101] Jarves, 390.

[102] *Id.*, 317.

[103] *Id.*, 321.

[104] Alexander, 226.

PART 2
Government Reform

CHAPTER 4
FORMALIZING HAWAIIAN LAW

*H*awaiian governance drew from political ideas of other countries as well as the experience of Hawaiian rulers. Hawai'i's history and circumstances were unique because Hawai'i did not experience the peasant uprisings and revolutions that occurred in Great Britain and France.[1] Legal cultures throughout Europe and the United States did, however, influence the leadership of the Hawaiian Kingdom, especially in the formative years of its transformation from absolute rule to constitutional governance.

Early in his reign, Kamehameha III's government stood upon the crumbling foundations of a feudal autocracy that could no longer handle the weight of geo-political and economic forces sweeping across the islands. Uniformity of law and the centralization of authority had

King Kamehameha III (Hawai'i Archives)

become a necessity. Increased commercial trade brought an influx of foreigners wishing to reside and conduct business in the Kingdom, requiring changes in the legal system. In 1831, British General William Miller made the following observation of Hawaiian governance at the time:

> *If then the natives wish to retain the government of the islands in their own hands and become a nation, if they are anxious to avoid being dictated to by any foreign commanding officer that may be sent to this station, it seems to be absolutely necessary that they should establish some defined form of government, and a few fundamental laws that will afford security for property; and such commercial regulations as will serve for their own guidance as well as for that of foreigners; if these regulations be liberal, as they ought to be, commerce will flourish, and all classes of people will be gainers.*[2]

Kamehameha III turned to his religious advisors—the missionaries—for advice. William Richards volunteered to travel to the United States in search of someone to instruct the chiefs on government reform. When Richards was unable to find an instructor he dedicated himself, at the urging of Kamehameha III, to instruct the chiefs on political economy and governance. Richards had no formal education in political science or law but relied on the work of the President of Brown

University, Francis Wayland. Wayland was interested in "defining the limits of government by developing a theory of contractual enactment of political society, which would be morally and logically binding and acceptable to all its members."[3]

Richards developed a curriculum based upon Hawaiian translations of Wayland's two books, "Elements of Moral Science (1835)" and "Elements of Political Economy (1837)." According to Richards, the "lectures themselves were mere outlines of general principles of political economy, which of course could not have been understood except by full illustration drawn from Hawaiian custom and Hawaiian circumstances."[4] Richards sought to theorize governance from a foundation of *natural rights* within an agrarian society based upon capitalism that was not only cooperative in nature, but also morally grounded in Christian values. His translation of Wayland's Elements of Political Economy, states "Peace and tranquility are not maintained when righteousness is not maintained. The righteousness of the chiefs and the people is the only basis for maintaining the laws of the government."[5] Laws should be enacted to maintain a society for the benefit of all and not the few.

William Richards
(Hawai'i Archives)

Richards asserted, "God did not establish man as servants for the chiefs and as a means for chiefs to become rich. God provided for the occupation of government leaders in order to bless the people and so that the nation benefits."[6] Wayland's theory of cooperative capitalism, with private ownership of land and a free market as the foundation of political economy, was difficult to implement because the Kingdom was in a feudal state since the rule of Kamehameha I. Individuals could not hold land titles in the form of freehold titles, e.g. fee-simple and life estates. Therefore, personal property and agriculture formed the basis of the Hawaiian economy at this stage. According to an 1840 statute,

> *The business of the Governors, and land agents [Konohiki], and tax officers of the general tax gatherer, is as follows: to read frequently this law to the people on all days of public work, and thus shall the landlords do in the presence of their tenants on their working days. Let every one also put his own land in a good state, with proper reference to the welfare of the body, according to the principles of Political Economy. The man who does not labor enjoys little happiness. He cannot obtain any great good unless he strives for it with earnestness. He cannot make himself comfortable, not even preserve his life unless he labor for it. If a man wish to become rich, he can do it in no way except to engage with energy in some business. Thus Kings obtain kingdoms by striving for them with energy."[7]*

CONSTITUTIONAL EVOLUTION

On June 7, 1839, Kamehameha III proclaimed an expanded uniform code of laws preceded by a "Declaration of Rights" that formally acknowledged and vowed to protect the *natural rights* of life, limb, and liberty for both chiefs and people. The code provided that "no chief has any authority over any man, any farther than it is given him by specific enactment, and no tax can be levied, other than that which is specified in the printed law, and no chief can act as a judge in a case where he is personally interested, and no man can be dispossessed of land which he has put under cultivation except for crimes specified in the law."[8] On October 8, 1840, Kamehameha III approved the first constitution incorporating the Declaration of Rights as its preamble.

The purpose of a written constitution was "to lay down the general features of a system of government and to define to a greater or less extent the powers of such government, in relation to the rights of persons on the one hand, and on the other...in relation to certain other political entities which are incorporated in the system."[9] The first constitution did not provide for separation of powers (e.g. executive, legislative and judicial). The King's duty was to execute the laws of the land, serve as chief judge of the Supreme Court, and sit as a member of the House of Nobles that would enact laws together with representatives chosen from the people. The first constitution was not a limitation of power, but a sharing of power. Kamehameha III declared and established the equality of all his subjects before the law and voluntarily divested himself of his power as an absolute Ruler.[10] According to the Hawaiian Supreme Court:

> *King Kamehameha III originally possessed, in his own person, all the attributes of absolute sovereignty. Of his own free will he granted the Constitution of 1840, as a boon to his country and people, establishing his Government upon a declared plan or system, having reference not only to the permanency of his Throne and Dynasty, but to the Government of his country according to fixed laws and civilized usage, in lieu of what may be styled the feudal, but chaotic and uncertain system, which previously prevailed.[11]*

The role of the Prime Minister established by Kamehameha I in 1794 was a misnomer. There were no other ministers that ran government by direction of a primary minister appointed by the Crown until 1845, when a cabinet ministry was established for the first time by statute.[12] Prior to 1845, Hawaiian governance did not experience, as the British did, the function of ministers in administering government separate from the Crown. According to Bryum Carter, a political scientist, the first prototype of the modern Prime Minister emerged during the reigns of the first two Hanoverian Kings, George I and II.[13] George I had little interest in English politics nor a grasp of the English language, and often returned to Hanover and left the country to be run by his cabinet ministers who were led by Sir Robert Walpole and Lord Charles Townshend. Shortly after the ascension of George II, Townshend resigned, and Walpole was able to gain full control of the cabinet ministry, thereby creating the office of Prime Minister that "made possible the evolution of the modern system of ministerial responsibility."[14]

The role of the Hawaiian Prime Minister (Kālaimoku) under Kamehameha I, was primarily as an agent at will of the Crown on matters of national governance. It was an idiosyncrasy of Hawaiian governance, that the title Prime Minister would be replaced with Premier (Kuhina Nui) after the death of Kamehameha I, because the term premier literally means the main or prime minister of a cabinet of ministers. According to the First Act of Kamehameha III, which was passed by the Hawaiian Legislature in 1845, the Premier, in addition to the duties enumerated in the Constitution, headed the cabinet ministry as Minister of the Interior and from this point on was a prime minister in the truest sense of the title. The duties of the Premier, as provided by constitutional provision includes:

> *All business connected with the special interests of the kingdom, which the King wishes to transact, shall be done by the Premier under the authority of the King. All documents and business of the kingdom executed by the Premier, shall be considered as executed by the King's authority. All government property shall be reported to him (or her) and he (or she) shall make it over to the King. The Premier shall be the King's special counselor in the great business of the kingdom. The King shall not act without the knowledge of the Premier, nor shall the Premier act without the knowledge of the King, and the veto of the King on the acts of the Premier shall arrest the business. All important business of the kingdom which the King chooses to transact in person, he may do it but not without the approbation of the Premier.*[15]

HAWAIIAN INDEPENDENCE AND THE QUESTION OF BRITISH SOVEREIGNTY

The only British policy regarding the kingdom appears to have been the meeting of the Sandwich Islands delegation with King George IV in 1824 and the secret instructions given to Lord Byron. But these instructions apparently were not communicated to Kamehameha III, Ka'ahumanu or the Council of Chiefs.

Lord Aberdeen

After French troops temporarily occupied the Hawaiian Kingdom in 1839 under the command of Captain Laplace, Lord Ingestre, a member of the British House of Commons, called upon the Secretary of State for Foreign Affairs, Viscount Palmerston, to provide an official response.[16] Viscount Palmerston reported he knew very little of the situation with the French, and with regard to the protectorate status of the Islands "he was non-committal and seemed to indicate that he knew very little about the subject."[17]

In the eyes of the Hawaiian government, Viscount Palmerston's report dispelled the notion of British dependency and acknowledged Hawaiian independence.[18] Two years later, a clearer British policy toward the Hawaiian Islands by Viscount Palmerston's successor, Lord Aberdeen, reinforced the position of the Hawaiian government. In a letter to the British Admiralty on October 4th 1842, Viscount Canning, on behalf of Lord Aberdeen, wrote:

Lord Aberdeen does not think it advantageous or politic, to seek to establish a paramount influence for Great Britain in those Islands, at the expense of that enjoyed by other Powers. All that appears to his Lordship to be required, is, that no other Power should exercise a greater degree of influence than that possessed by Great Britain.[19]

Timoteo Haʻalilio (Hawaiʻi Archives)

In the summer of 1842, Kamehameha III moved forward to secure the position of the Hawaiian Kingdom as a recognized independent state under international law. He sought the formal recognition of Hawaiian independence from the three naval powers of the world at the time—Great Britain, France, and the United States. To accomplish this, Kamehameha III commissioned three envoys, Timoteo Haʻalilio, William Richards, who at the time was still an American Citizen, and Sir George Simpson, a British subject. Of all three powers, it was the British that had a legal claim over the Hawaiian Islands through cession by Kamehameha I, but for political reasons the British could not openly exert its claim over the other two naval powers. Due to the islands prime economic and strategic location in the middle of the north Pacific, the political interest of all three powers was to ensure that none would have a greater interest than the other. This caused Kamehameha III "considerable embarrassment in managing his foreign relations, and…awakened the very strong desire that his Kingdom shall be formally acknowledged by the civilized nations of the world as a sovereign and independent State."[20]

While the envoys were on their diplomatic mission, a British Naval ship, HBMS *Carysfort*, under the command of Lord Paulet, entered Honolulu harbor on February 10, 1843, making outrageous demands on the Hawaiian government. Basing his actions on complaints made to him in letters from the British Consul, Richard Charlton, who was absent from the kingdom at the time, Paulet eventually seized control of the Hawaiian government on February 25, 1843, after threatening to level Honolulu with cannon fire.[21] Kamehameha III was forced to surrender the kingdom, but did so under written protest and pending the outcome of the mission of his diplomats in Europe. News of Paulet's action reached Admiral Richard Thomas of the British Admiralty, and he sailed from the Chilean

Lord Paulet (Hawaiʻi Archives)

port of Valparaiso and arrived in the islands on July 25, 1843. After a meeting with Kamehameha III, Admiral Thomas determined that Charlton's complaints did not warrant a British takeover and ordered the restoration of the Hawaiian government, which took place in a grand ceremony on July 31, 1843.[22] At a thanksgiving service after the ceremony, Kamehameha III proclaimed before a large crowd, *ua mau ke ea o ka 'āina i ka pono* (the life of the land is perpetuated in righteousness). The King's statement became the national motto.

The envoys eventually succeeded in getting formal international recognition of the Hawaiian Islands "as a sovereign and independent State." Great Britain and France formally recognized Hawaiian sovereignty on November 28, 1843 by joint proclamation at the Court of London, and the United States followed on July 6, 1844 by a letter of Secretary of State John C. Calhoun.[23] The Hawaiian Islands became the first Polynesian nation to be recognized as an independent and sovereign State. The Anglo-French proclamation stated:

> *Her Majesty the Queen of the United Kingdom of Great Britain and Ireland, and His Majesty the King of the French, taking into consideration the existence in the Sandwich Islands of a government capable of providing for the regularity of its relations with foreign nations, have thought it right to engage, reciprocally, to consider the Sandwich Islands [Hawaiian Islands] as an Independent State, and never to take possession, neither directly or under the title of Protectorate, or under any other form, of any part of the territory of which they are composed.*[24]

As a recognized sovereign and independent State, the Hawaiian Islands became a full member of the Universal Postal Union on January 1, 1882, maintained more than ninety consulates throughout the world,[25] and entered into extensive diplomatic and treaty relations with other States that included Austria-Hungary, Belgium, Bremen, Denmark, France, Germany, Great Britain, Hamburg, Italy, Japan, Netherlands, Portugal, Russia, Spain, Sweden-Norway, Switzerland and the United States.[26] The Hawaiian Kingdom entered into four treaties with the United States: 1849 Treaty of Friendship, Commerce and Navigation;[27] 1875 Treaty of Reciprocity;[28] 1883 Postal Convention Concerning Money Orders;[29] and the 1884 Supplementary Convention to the 1875 Treaty of Reciprocity.[30] The Hawaiian Kingdom was also recognized within the international community as a neutral State as expressly stated in treaties with the Kingdom of Spain in 1863 and the Kingdom of Sweden and Norway in 1852. Article XXVI of the 1863 Hawaiian-Spanish treaty, for example, provides:

> *All vessels bearing the flag of Spain, shall, in time of war, receive every possible protection, short of active hostility, within the ports and waters of the Hawaiian Islands, and Her Majesty the Queen of Spain engages to respect, in time of war the neutrality of the Hawaiian Islands, and to use her good offices with all the other powers having treaties with the same, to induce them to adopt the same policy toward the said Islands.*[31]

The British government praised Admiral Thomas' action and by formally recognizing Hawaiian independence, relinquished all legal claims over the Hawaiian Islands. As an independent State, the Hawaiian Kingdom continued to evolve as a constitutional monarchy as it kept up with the rapidly changing political, social and economic conditions.

In 1845, Kamehameha III refocused his attention on domestic affairs, and the organization and maintenance of the newly established constitutional monarchy. On October 29th, he commissioned Robert Wyllie of Scotland to be Minister of Foreign Affairs; G.P. Judd, a former missionary, as Minister of Finance; William Richards as Minister of Education; and John Ricord, as Attorney General. All were granted Hawaiian citizenship prior to their appointments. These appointments sparked controversy and renewed concerns of foreign takeover. Responding to a slew of appeals to remove these foreign advisors for native chiefs, Kamehameha III wrote the following letter that speaks to the tenor of the time and circumstances the kingdom faced:

> *Kind greetings to you with kindly greetings to the old men and women of my ancestors' time. I desire all the good things of the past to remain such as the good old law of Kamehameha that "the old women and the old men shall sleep in safety by the wayside," and to unite with them what is good under these new conditions in which we live. That is why I have appointed foreign officials, not out of contempt for the ancient wisdom of the land, but because my native helpers do not yet understand the laws of the great countries who are working with us. That is why I have dismissed them. I see that I must have new officials to help with the new system under which I am working for the good of the country and of the old men and women of the country. I earnestly desire to give places to the commoners and to the chiefs, as they are able to do the work connected with the office. The people who have learned the new ways I have retained. Here is the name of one of them, G.L. Kapeau, Secretary of the Treasury. He understands the work very well, and I wish there were more such men. Among the chiefs Leleiōhoku, Paki, and John Young [Keoniana] are capable of filling such places and they already have government offices, one of them over foreign officials. And as soon as the young chiefs are sufficiently trained I hope to give them the places. But they are not now able to become speakers in foreign tongues. I have therefore refused the letters of appeal to dismiss the foreign advisors, for those who speak only the Hawaiian tongue.*[32]

John Ricord arrived in the Hawaiian Islands from Oregon on February 27, 1844 and was later appointed Attorney General on March 9th. He was an attorney by trade and well versed in both the civil law of continental Europe and the common law of both Britain and the United States.[33] The kingdom was only in its fourth year of constitutional governance and the shortcomings of the first constitution began to show. One of Ricord's first tasks was to establish a diplomatic code for Kamehameha III and the Royal Court, which was based on the principles of the 1815 Vienna Conference.[34]

His second and more important task was to draft a code to re-organize the executive and judicial departments for submission to the Legislature for approval. In a report to the Legislature, Ricord concluded that, "there is an almost total deficiency of laws, suited to the Hawaiian Islands as a recognized nation in reciprocity with others so mighty, so enlightened and so well organized as Great Britain, France, the United States of America, and Belgium."[35] Ricord observed that, "the Constitution had not been carried into full effect [and] its provisions needed assorting and arranging into appropriate families, and prescribed machinery to render them effective."[36]

The underlying issue was which system of law should serve as a model: France and Belgium's governments based on a Civil or Roman law tradition; or Great Britain and the United States' tradition of Common law. Ricord explained:

> The laws of Rome, that government from which all other governments of Europe, Western Asia and Africa descended, could not be used for Hawai'i, nor could those of England, France or any other country. The Hawaiian people must have laws adapted to their mode of living. But it is right to study the laws of other peoples, and fitting that those who conduct law offices in Hawai'i should understand these other laws and compare them to see which are adapted to our way of living and which are not.[37]

Complying with a legislative resolution, Ricord's draft code was based on a hybrid of both civil and common law.[38] Because the Hawaiian Islands were at the international crossroads of trade and commerce across the Pacific Ocean, merchants from many countries had influenced the evolution of Hawaiian law. Governmental organization leaned toward the principles of English and American common law, infused with some civil law, but at the very core was distinctively Hawaiian.

CHAPTER 5
CONSTITUTIONAL CHANGES

*I*n 1851, the Legislature passed a resolution calling for the appointment of three commissioners to propose amendments to the first Constitution of 1840. One was to be chosen by the King, one by the Nobles, and one by the Representatives. Elected Representative William Little Lee headed the commission and followed the structure and organization of the 1780 Massachusetts Constitution, the most advanced of any constitution at that time. It was organized into four parts: a preamble; a declaration of rights; a framework of government describing the legislative, executive and judicial branches; and an amendment article. The revised Hawaiian Constitution was submitted to the Legislature and approved by both the House of Nobles and the House of Representatives, and signed into law by the King on June 14, 1852.[39]

The amended constitution was similar in structure to the Massachusetts Constitution, but with a different order: a declaration of rights; a framework of government that described the functions of the executive subdivided into five sections, the legislative and judicial powers; and an article describing the mode of amending the constitution.

The theory of a constitutional monarchy states the "three powers of a modern [constitutional monarchy] have distinct functions, but are not completely separate. As part of an interdependent whole, each power is defined not only by its own particular function, but also by the other powers which limit and interact with it."[40] The revised constitution retained remnants of

centralized rule, giving the Crown the authority to alter the constitution or even cede the kingdom to a foreign state without legislative approval. These provisions would allow the King to
act swiftly if circumstances demanded. In particular, these provisions of the 1852 constitution
included:

> *Article 39. The King, by and with the approval of His Cabinet and Privy Council, in case of
> invasion or rebellion, can, place the whole Kingdom, or any part of it under martial law;
> and he can ever alienate it, if indispensable to free it from the insult and oppression of
> any foreign power.*

> *Article 45. All important business for the Kingdom which the King chooses to transact in
> person, he may do, but not without the approbation of the Kuhina Nui. The King and
> Kuhina Nui shall have a negative on each other's public acts.*

TENSIONS WITH FRANCE

These provisions were retained particularly because the Hawaiian Government had tenuous
relations with France since 1839, when French Captain Laplace coerced payment of $20,000.00
from Kamehameha III as insurance to prevent the persecution of Catholics. Laplace also forced
the King to sign another treaty imposing jury selection benefits to Frenchmen and a fixed duty
on French wine and brandies. On March 21, 1846, French Rear Admiral Hamelin, arriving on the
frigate *Virgini*, returned the four boxes containing the $20,000.00 to the Hawaiian government.[41]
Three days later on March 24th, Kamehameha III reluctantly signed two identical treaties with the
French and British that reiterated the Laplace's treaty provisions. These treaties superseded the
British 1836 treaty and the French 1839 treaty, and contained "two objectionable clauses, which
proved to be a source of trouble in subsequent years."[42]

> *Article III. No British [French] subject accused of any crime whatever shall be judged
> otherwise than by a jury composed of native or foreign residents, proposed the British
> [French] Consul and accepted by the Government of the Sandwich Islands.*

> *Article VI. British [French] merchandise or goods recognized as coming from the British
> [French] dominions, shall not be prohibited, nor shall they be subject to an import duty
> higher than five per cent ad valorem. Wines, brandies, and other spirituous liquors are
> however excepted from the stipulation, and shall be liable to such reasonable duty as the
> Hawaiian Government may think; fit to lay upon them, provided always that the amount
> of duty shall not be so high as absolutely to prohibit the importation of the said articles.*

In August 1849, French Consul Dillon accused the Hawaiian government of violating the 1846
French treaty. French Admiral Legoarant de Tromelin "sent the king a peremptory dispatch
containing ten demands which had been drawn up by Mr. Dillon."[43] These demands centered
on the treatment of Catholics, the duty on liquors, and the unequal treatment of Frenchmen. The
Hawaiian Government sent a courteous, yet firm, reply explaining that it had not violated the
treaty and that if any rights of French citizens have been violated,

the courts of the kingdom were open for the redress of all such grievances, and that until justice had been denied by them there could be no occasion for diplomatic interference. The government offered to refer any dispute to the mediation of a neutral power, and informed the admiral that no resistance would be made to the force at his disposal, and that in any event the persons and property of French residents would be scrupulously guarded.[44]

Nevertheless, Admiral De Tromelin landed an armed force in Honolulu and captured the government fort, "the customhouse and other government buildings, and seized the king's yacht, together with seven merchant vessels in port.[45] The fort had previously been abandoned and the Hawaiian Government provided no opposition. By proclamation of the Admiral on August 30, 1849, the ten-day occupation and the destruction of the fort were justified under France's international right of reprisal, and private property seized would be returned.

The two French warships left Honolulu for San Francisco on September 5, 1849, with the French consul Dillon and his family. Louis Perrin replaced Dillon as French Consul and arrived in Honolulu on December 13, 1850. To the Government's surprise, the new French Consul presented the same demands and continued the "policy of an annoying diplomatic interference with the internal affairs of the kingdom."[46] As a result, the King and Premier placed the kingdom temporarily under the protection of the United States, which ended the hostility of the French Consul.[47]

These events and other threats alarmed the King and other governmental officials and they considered ceding the Hawaiian Islands to the United States. By 1853, the topic of annexation to the United States was under serious deliberation by the King who "was tired of demands made upon him by foreign powers, and of threats by filibusters from abroad and by conspirators at home to overturn the government.[48] On February 16, 1854, the King "commanded Mr. Wyllie [Minister of Foreign Affairs] to ascertain on what terms a treaty of annexation could be negotiated, to be used as a safeguard to meet any sudden emergency."[49]

Negotiations between Wyllie and the American commissioner David L. Gregg were not successful and the discussions of annexation ended with the death of Kamehameha III on December 15, 1854. Despite open threats to the kingdom, Kamehameha III successfully transformed Hawaiian governance from a feudal autocracy to a constitutional government that recognized a uniform rule of law, and acknowledged and protected the rights of its citizenry.

The age of Kamehameha III was that of progress and of liberty—of schools and of civilization. He gave us a Constitution and fixed laws; he secured the people in the title to their lands, and removed the last chain of oppression. He gave them a voice in his councils and in the making of the laws by which they are governed. He was a great national benefactor, and has left the impress of his mild and amiable disposition on the age for which he was born.[50]

King Kamehameha IV (Hawai'i Archives)

Alexander Liholiho, the adopted son of the King, was confirmed successor on April 6th 1853, in accordance with Article 25 of the Constitution of 1852.[51] In 1854, after the death of the King, he succeeded to the throne as Kamehameha IV. Article 25 provided that the "successor [of the Throne] shall be the person whom the King and the House of Nobles shall appoint and publicly proclaim as such, during the King's life."

In the first year of his reign, Kamehameha IV approved an Act to separate the office of Kuhina Nui from that of Minister of Interior Affairs, also known as Minister of the Interior. The legislature reasoned that the "Kuhina Nui is invested by the Constitution with extraordinary powers, and whereas the public exigencies may require his release from the labor, and responsibilities of the office of Minister of Interior Affairs, now by law imposed upon him."[52]

In 1855, the Department of Public Instruction was established, by statute, replacing the Ministry of Public Instruction whose minister formerly served as a member of the cabinet council. This independent department was headed by a President who presided over a five-member Board of Education that was "superintended and directed by a committee of the Privy Council."[53]

At this point in time, the cabinet consisted of the Minister of the Interior, Minister of Finance, Minister of Foreign Affairs, and the Attorney General.[54] It was also the "duty of the Board

Kuhina Nui - Victoria Kamāmalu (Hawai'i Archives)

of Education, every sixth year, counting from the year 1860, to make a complete census of the inhabitants of the Kingdom, to be laid before the King and Legislature for their consideration."[55] The constitution was also amended in 1856, changing legislative sessions from annual to biennial. Kamehameha IV sought to eliminate the sovereign prerogatives by constitutional amendment, but was unsuccessful. The responsibility for such change would fall on his successor and brother, Lot Kapuaiwa.

On November 30th 1863, Kamehameha IV died unexpectedly, and left the Kingdom without a successor.[56] On the same day, the Premier, Victoria Kamāmalu, in Privy Council, proclaimed Lot Kapuaiwa to be the successor to the throne in accordance with Article 25 of the Constitution of 1852, and the Nobles confirmed him. Lot Kapuaiwa was thereafter called

Kamehameha V. Article 47, of the Constitution of 1852, provided that "whenever the throne shall become vacant by reason of the King's death the Kuhina Nui shall perform all the duties incumbent on the King, and shall have and exercise all the powers, which by this Constitution are vested in the King."

Victoria Kamāmalu provided continuity for the office of the Crown pending the appointment and confirmation of Lot Kapuaiwa. Upon his ascension, Kamehameha V refused to take the oath of office until the 1852 Constitution was altered in order to remove those sovereign prerogatives that ran contrary to the principles of a constitutional monarchy, namely articles 45 and 94.[57]

King Kamehameha V (Hawai'i Archives)

Kamehameha V knew that he had a choice not to take the oath, and that his refusal to take the oath was constitutionally authorized by article 94 of the Constitution, which provided that the "King, after approving this Constitution, shall take the following oath." Since he did not approve the Constitution, he was not required to take the oath. Kamehameha V felt the constitutional provisions should be changed since they were a source of great difficulty for his late brother Kamehameha IV, and would continue to be problematic for him and the Legislative Assembly. If he did take the oath, he would have bound himself to the constitution whereby any change or amendment to the constitution was vested solely with the Legislative Assembly. By not taking the oath, he reserved for himself the responsibility of change, which ironically was authorized by the very constitution he sought to amend.

1864 CONSTITUTION

Kamehameha V and his predecessor recognized articles 45 and 94 as a hindrance to responsible government, and therefore he convened the first Constitutional Convention to draft a new constitution on July 7, 1864.[58] Between July 7 and August 8, 1864, each article in the proposed constitution was read and discussed until the Convention arrived at article 62. The King and Nobles wanted to insert property qualifications for representatives and voters, but the elected delegates refused. After days of debate over article 62, the Convention was deadlocked. As a result, Kamehameha V, in an act of irony, dissolved the convention and exercised his sovereign prerogative under article 45, and he annulled the 1852 constitution and proclaimed a new constitution on August 20, 1864.

In his speech at the opening of the Legislative Assembly of 1864, Kamehameha V explained his action by making specific reference to the "forty-fifth article [that] reserved to the Sovereign the right to conduct personally, in cooperation with the Kuhina Nui (Premier), but without the intervention of a Ministry or the approval of the Legislature, such portions of the public business as he might choose to undertake."[59] The constitution was not new, but rather the same draft that was before the convention with the exception of the property qualifications for Representatives and voters as embodied in Articles 61 and 62.

> *Article 61: No person shall be eligible for a Representative of the People, who is insane or an idiot; nor unless he be a male subject of the Kingdom, who shall have arrived at the full age of Twenty-One years—who shall know how to read and write—who shall understand accounts—and shall have been domiciled in the Kingdom for at least three years, the last of which shall be the year immediately preceding his election; and who shall own Real Estate, within the Kingdom, of a clear value, over and above all incumbrances, of at least Five Hundred Dollars; or who shall have an annual income of at least Two Hundred and Fifty Dollars; derived from any property, or some lawful employment.*

> *Article 62: "Every male subject of the Kingdom, who shall have paid his taxes, who shall have attained the age of twenty years, and shall have been domiciled in the Kingdom for one year immediately preceding the election; and shall be possessed of Real Property in this Kingdom, to the value over and above all incumbrances of One Hundred and Fifty Dollars or a Lease-hold property on which the rent is Twenty-five Dollars per year—or of an income of not less than Seventy-five Dollars per year, derived from any property or some lawful employment, and shall know how to read and write, if born since the year 1840, and shall have caused his name to be entered on the list of voters of his District as may be provided by law, shall be entitled to one vote for the Representative or Representatives of that District. Provided, however, that no insane or idiotic person, nor any person who shall have been convicted of any infamous crime within this Kingdom, unless he shall have been pardoned by the King, and by the terms of such pardon have been restored to all the rights of a subject, shall be allowed to vote."*

The office of Premier was also eliminated under the new constitution, which also provided that no act of the Crown was valid unless countersigned by a responsible Minister from the Cabinet, who answered to the Legislative Assembly and could be removed by a vote of a lack of confidence or impeachment proceedings.

The function of the Privy Council was greatly reduced, and a Regency replaced the function of Premier if the King died, leaving a minor heir, who would "administer the Government in the name of the King, and exercise all the powers which are Constitutionally vested in the King."[60] The Crown was bound to take the oath of office upon ascension to the throne, and the Legislative Assembly had the sole authority to amend or alter the constitution. The Legislative Assembly was now a unicameral body comprised of appointed Nobles and Representatives elected by the people. The constitution also provided that the "Supreme Power of the

Kingdom in its exercise, is divided into the Executive, Legislative, and Judicial; these shall always be preserved distinct."[61] Thus, the separation of powers doctrine was fully enshrined in Hawaiian constitutional governance.

The 1864 Legislative Assembly appointed a special committee comprised of Godfrey Rhodes, John Iʻi, and J.W.H. Kauwahi to respond to Kamehameha V's opening speech of the new legislature. The committee recognized the constitutionality of the King's prerogative under the former constitution and acknowledged that this "prerogative converted into a right by the terms of the [1852] Constitution, Your Majesty has now parted with, both for Yourself and Successors, and this Assembly thoroughly recognizes the sound judgment by which Your Majesty was actuated in the abandonment of a privilege, which, at some future time might have been productive of untold evil to the nation."[62] The Crown was not only authorized by law to do what had been done, but the action of Kamehameha V further limited his own authority under the former constitution. He was the last Monarch to exercise absolutism.

King Lunalilo (Hawaiʻi Archives)

On December 11, 1872, Kamehameha V died without naming a successor to the throne, and the Legislative Assembly, empowered to elect a new monarch under the 1864 Constitution, elected William Charles Lunalilo on January 8, 1873.

The Hawaiian Kingdom's first elected King died a year later without a named successor, and the Legislature elected David Kalākaua as King on February 12, 1874. During this special session, the Legislative Assembly also repealed the property qualifications embodied in articles 61 and 62 of the constitution, but maintained the literacy qualification. On February 14, 1874, King Kalākaua appointed his younger brother, Prince William Pitt Leleiōhoku, his successor, but Leleiōhoku died April 10, 1877. The next day the King appointed his sister, Princess Liliʻuokalani, as heir apparent and received confirmation from the Nobles.

When Kalākaua was elected, a new royal lineage replaced the Kamehameha dynasty. Princess Liliʻuokalani, Queen Kapiʻolani, Princess Virginia Kapoʻoloku Poʻomaikelani, Princess Kinoiki, Princess Victoria Kawekiu Kaiʻulani Lunalilo Kalaninuiahilapalapa, Prince David Kawānanakoa, Prince Edward Abner Keliʻiahonui, and Prince Jonah Kūhiō Kalanianaʻole comprised the new royal lineage.

On August 9, 1880, a Board of Genealogists of Hawaiian Chiefs was established by law to "collect from genealogical books, and from the knowledge of old people the history and genealogy of the Hawaiian chiefs, and shall publish a book."[63] The Board was also tasked with the duty of "establishing the arms and insignia of chief families, searching for ancient relics which have been lost or concealed in places of concealment, and for ascertaining and preserving from violation the ancient places of sepulture of the chiefs."[64]   The preamble of the statute states:

Whereas, it is provided by the 22d article of the Constitution that the Kings of Hawaii shall be chosen from the native chiefs of the Kingdom; and whereas, at the present day it is difficult to ascertain who are the chiefs, as contemplated by said article of the Constitution, and it is proper that such genealogies of the Kingdom be perpetuated, and also the history of the chiefs and kings from ancient times down to the present day, which would also be a guide to the King in the appointment of Nobles in the Legislative Assembly.[65]

CHAPTER 6
REVOLT

King Kalākaua (Hawai'i Archives)

During the summer of 1887, while the Legislature was out of session, a minority of subjects of the Hawaiian Kingdom and foreign nationals met to organize a revolt and take over the government. The driving motivation was their belief that the "native [was] unfit for government and his power must be curtailed."[66] The local volunteer militia, predominantly United States citizens, called themselves the Hawaiian League, and held a meeting on June 30, 1887 at the Armory building of the Honolulu Rifles. Before this meeting, members of the League had brought large caches of arms from San Francisco and distributed them to other members.[67]

The group made demands on Kalākaua, including an immediate change of the King's cabinet ministers. Under threat of violence, on July 1, 1887, the King reluctantly agreed to form a new cabinet ministry made up of League members. The true purpose of the League was to neutralize the power of the native vote in order to seize control of the government for their economic gain.

On that same day, the new cabinet comprised of William L. Green as Minister of Finance, Godfrey Brown as Minister of Foreign Affairs, Lorrin A. Thurston as Minister of the Interior, and Clarence W. Ashford as Attorney General, took "an oath to support the Constitution and Laws, and faithfully and impartially to discharge the duties of his office."[68]   Under strict secrecy and unbeknownst to Kalākaua, the new ministry also invited two members of the Supreme Court, Chief Justice Albert F. Judd and Associate Justice Edward Preston, "to assist in the preparation of a new constitution,"[69] on July 5, 1887, consequently implicating the two highest ranking judicial officers in the revolt. The Chief Justice had the following document acknowledged and signed:[70]

> *Messrs. S.B. Dole and W.O. Smith and W.A. Kinney, having waited upon the undersigned with a draft of a proposed new Constitution, and having requested us to peruse the same and advise with them as to the form and text of the same, hereby state that we do so under the express understanding that we cannot and do not assent to any change in the present Constitution or to the promulgation of any new Constitution unless made in conformity with the provisions of the Constitution now in force, we having been sworn to maintain that constitution and the laws of the Kingdom and our duty being to maintain such laws, but it being presented to us that the promulgation of a new Constitution is imperatively necessary to maintain peace and order I agree to advise with such gentlemen for the purposes aforesaid.*

> [Signed]
> *A.F. Judd*
> *Edward Preston*

> [Signed]
> *S.B. Dole*
> *William O. Smith*
> *W.A. Kinney*

Hawaiian constitutional law provided that any proposed change to the constitution must be submitted to the Legislative Assembly, and upon majority agreement, would be deferred to the next legislative session for action.[71] Once the next legislature convened, and the proposed amendment or amendments were "agreed to by two-thirds of all members of the Legislative Assembly, and be approved by the King, such amendment or amendments shall become part of the Constitution of this country."[72]

As a minority, these individuals had no intent of submitting their draft constitution to the legislature, which was not scheduled to reconvene until 1888. Instead, they embarked on a criminal path of treason. The Penal Code defines *treason* "to be any plotting or attempt to dethrone or destroy the King, or the levying of war against the King's government…the same being done by a person owing allegiance to this kingdom. Allegiance is the obedience and fidelity due to the kingdom from those under its protection."[73] The statute also states when actions:

> *constitute the levying of war, the force must be employed or intended to be employed for the dethroning or destruction of the King or in contravention of the laws, or in opposition to the authority of the King's government, with an intent or for an object affecting some of the branches or departments of said government generally, or affecting the enactment, repeal or enforcement of laws in general, or of some general law; or affecting the people,*

or the public tranquility generally; in distinction from some special intent or object affecting individuals other than the King, or a particular district.[74]

THE BAYONET CONSTITUTION

Chief Justice Albert Judd (Hawai'i Archives)

The draft constitution was completed on the afternoon of July 5, 1887 and Chief Justice Judd was called in to swear the King to the new constitution in the presence of the Cabinet. But before he signed it, the King asked Judd if he should carry through with his signature. Judd replied, "You must follow the advice of your responsible ministers."[75] Kalākaua did not know that the highest judicial officer was a co-conspirator. The 1887 Constitution was declared to be the new law of the land. The King's sister and heir-apparent, Lili'uokalani, discovered later that her brother had signed the constitution "because he had every assurance, short of actual demonstration, that the conspirators were ripe for revolution, and had taken measures to have him assassinated if he refused."[76] Charles Gulick, who served as Minister of the Interior from 1883 to 1886, also concluded:

The ready acquiescence of the King to their demands seriously disconcerted the conspirators, as they had hoped that his refusal would have given them an excuse for deposing him, and a show of resistance a justification for assassinating him. Then everything would have been plain sailing for their little oligarchy, with a sham republican constitution.[77]

This constitution, known as the Bayonet Constitution, was never submitted to the Legislative Assembly. It was drafted by a select group of twenty individuals[78] and effectively placed control of the Legislature and Cabinet in the hands of individuals who held foreign allegiances.

The constitution maintained a unicameral legislature, but the election of Nobles replaced appointments by the King. Property qualifications were reinstituted for candidates of both Nobles and Representatives. And the cabinet could only be removed by the legislature by a vote of lack of confidence. The new property qualifications ensured that Nobles would be non-natives and would control the elected Representatives.

For the first time in the history of the country the number of nobles is made equal to the number of representatives. This furnished a veto power over the representatives of the popular vote to the nobles, who were selected by persons mostly holding foreign allegiance, and not subjects of the Kingdom. The election of a single representative by the foreign element gave to it the legislature.[79]

The resident foreigners of American or European nationality were allowed to cast their votes in the election of the new legislature without renouncing their foreign citizenship and allegiance. The resident foreigners included contract laborers from Portugal's Madeira and Azores Islands who emigrated to the kingdom after 1878 under labor contracts for the sugar plantations owned by League members. Although few of these workers could read or write, League members utilized this large voting block to neutralize the native vote. According to James Blount, Special Commissioner:

These ignorant laborers were taken before the election from the cane fields in large numbers by the overseer before the proper officer to administer the oath and then carried to the polls and voted according to the will of the plantation manager. Why was this done? In the language of the Chief Justice Judd, "to balance the native vote with the Portuguese vote." This same purpose is admitted by all persons here. Again, large numbers of Americans, Germans, English, and other foreigners unnaturalized were permitted to vote...[80]

Leading up to the elections on September 12th, there was public outcry.[81] On August 30th 1887, British Consul Wodehouse reported to the British government the new Cabinet's response: "The new Administration which was dictated by the "Honolulu Rifles" now 300 strong does not give universal satisfaction, and...Attorney General Ashford is reported to have said 'that they, the Administration, would carry the elections if necessary at the point of the bayonet.'"[82]

The election "took place with the foreign population well armed and the troops hostile to the crown and people."[83] James Blount also concluded that foreign ships anchored in Honolulu harbor during this time "must have restrained the native mind or indeed any mind from a resort to physical force," and the natives' "means of resistance was naturally what was left of political power."[84]

Unlike Kamehameha V, Kalākaua, as the chief executive, did not have the constitutional authority to abrogate and then subsequently promulgate a new constitution without legislative approval. The constitution of 1864 no longer had the sovereign prerogative of Article 45, thus the Crown was limited to faithfully executing Hawaiian law as the country's chief executive.

Further restraint against sovereign authority was that the enactment of law, whether constitutional or statutory, resided solely with the Legislative Assembly together with the Crown. Article 78 of the 1864 Constitution provided that all "laws now in force in this Kingdom, shall continue and remain in full effect, until altered or repealed by the Legislature; such parts only excepted as are repugnant to this Constitution. All laws heretofore enacted, or that may hereafter be enacted, which are contrary to this Constitution, shall be null and void."

RESISTANCE BY THE HAWAIIAN CITIZENRY

Throughout the revolt, there was active opposition to the minority of insurgents by the Hawaiian citizenry that ranged from peaceful organized resistance to unsuccessful armed attacks. On November 22, 1888, the Hawaiian Political Association (Hui Kālai'āina) was established with the purpose of "restoration of the constitutional system existing before June 30, 1887."[85] For the next five years this organization was the most persistent and influential in maintaining that the constitution of 1864, as amended, was the legal constitution of the country.

Robert Wilcox (Hawai'i Archives)

In June 1889, the Liberal Patriotic Association, a secret society, was formed "to restore the former system of government and the former rights of the king."[86] The following month on July 30th, the organization's leader, Robert Wilcox, led an unsuccessful armed attack with 80 men against the cabinet ministry on the grounds of 'Iolani Palace. Wilcox was initially indicted for treason, "but it became clear that...no native jury would convict him of that crime. The treason charge was dropped and he was brought to trial on an indictment for conspiracy."[87] He was tried by a native jury, which found him not guilty. Their verdict represented the native sentiment throughout the kingdom, representing eighty-five percent of the Hawaiian citizenry. In a dispatch to U.S. Secretary of State James Blaine on November 4, 1889, U.S. Minister John Stevens from the American legation in Honolulu acknowledged the significance of the verdict:

This preponderance of native opinion in favor of Wilcox, as expressed by the native jury, fairly represented the popular native sentiment throughout these islands in regard to his effort to overthrow the present ministry and to change the constitution of 1887, so as to restore to the King the power he possessed under the former constitution.[88]

There is a strong argument that the actions taken by Wilcox and other members of the Liberal Patriotic Association was a lawful but unsuccessful citizen's arrest, and not a counter-revolt as characterized by the cabinet ministry. In theory, a counter-revolt can only take place if the original revolt was successful. But if the original revolt was not successful, or in other words, the country was still in a state of revolt or unlawfulness, any action taken to apprehend or to hold accountable the original perpetrators is not a violation of the law, but rather an enforcement of the law. Under the common law, every private "person that is present when any felony is committed, is bound by the law to arrest the felon."[89]

According to the Hawaiian Penal Code, the "terms felony and crime, are...synonymous, and mean such offenses as are punishable with death," which makes treason a felony. Therefore, Wilcox's attack should be considered a failed attempt to apprehend insurgents serving in the cabinet ministry. Wilcox reinforced the theory of citizen's arrest when he lashed out at Lorrin Thurston on the floor of the Legislative Assembly in 1890. Thurston, one of the organizers of the 1887 revolt, was an insurgent who served at the time as the Minister of the Interior.

> *Yes, Mr. Minister, with your heart ever full of venom for the people and country which nurtured you and your fathers, I say, you and such as you are the murderers. The murderers and the blood of the murdered should be placed where it belongs, with those who without warrant opened fire upon natives trying to secure a hearing of their grievances before their King.... Our object was to restore a portion of the rights taken away by force of arms from the King.... Before the Living God, I never felt this action of mine to be a rebellion against my mother land, her independence, and her rights, but (an act) for the support and strengthening of the rights of my beloved race, the rights of liberty, the rights of the Throne and the good of the beautiful flag of Hawai'i; and if I die as a result of this my deed, it is a death of which I will be most proud, and I have hope I will never lack the help of the Heavens until all the rights are returned which have been snatched by the self-serving migrants of America.[90]*

Queen Lili'uokalani (Hawai'i Archives)

At the close of this tumultuous 1890 legislative session, where Hawaiian subjects stated their objections, the King's health had deteriorated. On November 25th he departed for San Francisco on board the *USS Charleston* for a period of respite and designated Lili'uokalani, his heir apparent, as Regent during his absence. King Kalākaua died in San Francisco on January 20, 1891, and his body returned to Honolulu on board the USS Charleston on the 29th.

In a meeting of the Privy Council that afternoon, Lili'uokalani took the oath of office, where she swore "in the presence of Almighty God, to maintain the Constitution of the Kingdom whole and inviolate, and to govern in conformity therewith." Chief Justice Albert F. Judd administered the oath and Lili'uokalani was thereafter proclaimed Queen.

The legislative and judicial branches of government had been compromised by the revolt. The Nobles became an elected body of men whose allegiance was to the foreign population, and three of the justices of the Supreme Court, including the Chief Justice, participated in the revolt by drafting the 1887 constitution. The Queen was prevented from legally confirming her niece, Ka'iulani Cleghorn, as heir-apparent, because the Nobles had not been in the

Legislative Assembly since 1887. Article 22 of the Constitution provides that "the successor shall be the person whom the Sovereign shall appoint with the consent of the Nobles, and publicly proclaim as such during the King's life."

Nevertheless, Ka'iulani, by nomination of the Queen, could be considered a *de facto* heir-apparent, subject to confirmation by the Nobles when they reconvened. Despite the ongoing political turmoil in the Hawaiian Kingdom, preparations were being made to celebrate fifty years of Hawaiian independence since the Anglo-French proclamation of November 28th 1843. The year 1893 marked the fiftieth anniversary of Hawai'i as an internationally recognized independent and sovereign State.

KEY CONCEPTS

Constitution	Government Reform	Natural Rights
Constitutionalism	Separation of Power	Revolt

FURTHER CONSIDERATION

1. What were the driving factors that caused Kamehameha III to initiate government reform? Break out into groups to discuss what were those factors and ask yourself, "Could I have done a better job, given Hawaiian governance at the time and the circumstances of foreign presence?"

2. Was it legal for Kamehameha V to abrogate the 1852 Constitution and replace it with a new constitution? Explain the circumstances that led up to this action and answer whether or not Kalākaua could do the same when the Bayonet Constitution was signed by the King on July 6, 1887.

3. How did the role of Prime Minister change before and after the 1864 Constitution?

[1] Hawaiian history finds no comparison to political philosophers like John Locke and Jean-Jacques Rousseau's social contract theory that recognized popular sovereignty in the people.

[2] Ralph S. Kuykendall, *The Hawaiian Kingdom: 1778-1854, Foundation and Transformation*, vol. 1 (University of Hawai'i Press, 1938), 122.

[3] Juri Mykkanen, *Inventing Politics: A New Political Anthropology of the Hawaiian Kingdom*, (University of Hawai'i Press, 2003), 154.

[4] William Richards, "William Richard's Report to the Sandwich Islands Mission on His First Year In Government Service, 1838-1839," *Fifty-first Annual Report of the Hawaiian Historical Society for the Year 1942* (Hawaiian Printing Company, Limited, 1943), 66.

[5] William Richards, *No ke Kālai'āina* (Lahaina: Lahainaluna High School Press, 1840), 123. "Aole hoi e mau ka malu ana a me ka kuapapa nui ana o ka aina ke malama ole ia ka pono. O ka pono o na 'lii a me na kanaka, o ia wale no ke kumu e paa ai na kanawai a me ke aupuni." Translation by Keao NeSmith, University of Hawai'i at Manoa.

[6] *Id.*, 64. "Aole i hoonoho mai ke Akua i na kanaka i poe hana na na 'lii a i mea e waiwai ai na 'lii. Ua haawi mai ke Akua i ka oihana alii mea e pomaikai ai na kanaka i mea hoi e pono ai ka aina." Translation by Keao NeSmith, University of Hawai'i at Manoa.

[7] William Richards, Translation of the Constitution and Laws of the Hawaiian Islands, established in the reign of Kamehameha III (Lahainaluna, 1842), 28. The quoted text is a translation from the Hawaiian text of Richards' No Ke Kālai'āina, 127.

[8] *Id.*, 68.

[9] Edward S. Corwin, "Constitution v. Constitutional Theory," *The American Political Science Review* 19(2) (1925): 290-304, 291.

[10] *In the Matter of the Estate of His Majesty Kamehameha IV*, 3 Hawai'i 715, 720 (1864).

[11] *Rex v. Joseph Booth*, 3 Hawai'i 616, 630 (1863).

[12] *Statute Laws of His Majesty Kamehameha III*, vol. 1 (Government Press, 1846), 2.

[13] Bryum Carter, *The Office of Prime Minister* (Princeton University Press, 1956), 22.

[14] A.B. Keith, *The King and the Imperial Crown* (Longman, Green and Co., 1936), 64.

[15] 1840 Constitution.

[16] He also "desired to be informed whether those islands which, in the year 1794, and subsequently in the year 1824,…had been declared to be under the protection of the British Government, were still considered…to remain in the same position." Kuykendall, vol. 1, 185.

[17] *Id.*

[18] *Report of the Minister of Foreign Affairs*, May 21, 1845 (Polynesian Press 1845), 7.

[19] *Report of the Historical Commission of the Territory of Hawai'i for the two years ending December 31, 1824* (Star-Bulletin, Ltd 1925), 36.

[20] United States House of Representatives, 53rd Congress, Executive Documents on Affairs in Hawaii: 189-95, 42 (Government Printing Office 1895) [hereafter Executive Documents].

[21] Kuykendall, vol. 1, 214.

[22] *Id.*, 220.

[23] *Report of the Minister of Foreign Affairs*, 4.

[24] Executive Documents, 120. Reprinted in *Hawaiian Journal of Law & Politics* 1 (Summer 2004): 114.

[25] Hawaiian Almanac, "Hawaiian Register and Directory for 1893," (Thos. G. Thrum 1892): 140.

[26] These treaties, except for the 1875 Hawaiian-Austro/Hungarian treaty, which is at the Hawai'i Archives, can be found in *Treaties and Conventions Concluded Between the Hawaiian Kingdom and other Power, since 1825* (Elele Book, Card and Job Print 1887): Belgium (Oct. 4, 1862) at 71; Bremen (March 27, 1854) at 43; Denmark (Oct. 19, 1846) at 11; France (July 17, 1839, March 26, 1846, September 8, 1858), at 5, 7 and 57; French Tahiti (Nov. 24, 1853) at 41; Germany (March 25, 1879) at 129; Great Britain (Nov. 13, 1836 and March 26, 1846) at 3 and 9; Great Britain's New South Wales (March 10, 1874) at

119; Hamburg (Jan. 8, 1848) at 15; Italy (July 22, 1863) at 89; Japan (Aug. 19, 1871, January 28, 1886) at 115 and 147; Netherlands (Oct. 16, 1862) at 79; Portugal (May 5, 1882) at 143; Russia (June 19, 1869) at 99; Samoa (March 20, 1887) at 171; Spain (Oct. 9, 1863) at 101; Sweden and Norway (April 5, 1855) at 47; and Switzerland (July 20, 1864) at 83.

[27] 9 U.S. Stat. 977. Reprinted at *Hawaiian Journal of Law & Politics* 1 (Summer 2004): 115-125.

[28] 19 U.S. Stat. 625. Reprinted at *Hawaiian Journal of Law & Politics* 1 (Summer 2004): 126-128.

[29] 23 U.S. Stat. 736. Reprinted at *Hawaiian Journal of Law & Politics* 1 (Summer 2004): 129-133.

[30] 25 U.S. Stat. 1399. Reprinted at *Hawaiian Journal of Law & Politics* 1 (Summer 2004): 134-135.

[31] Elele, 1863 *Spanish Treaty*, 108.

[32] Samuel M. Kamakau, *Ruling Chiefs of Hawai'i* (Kamehameha Schools Press 1992), 401.

[33] Chief Justice Judd stated that Ricord "seems to have been learned in the civil as well as the common law, as a consequence, no doubt, of his residence in Louisiana." A.F. Judd, "Early Constitution of the Judiciary of the Hawaiian Islands," *Maile Wreath*, February 1875, reprinted in *Hawaiian Almanac and Annual* (Press Publishing Company Steam Print, 1888), 65.

[34] "Besides prescribing rank orders, the mode of applying for royal audience, and the appropriate dress code, the new court etiquette set the Hawaiian standard for practically everything that constituted the royal symbolism" Juri Mykkanen, *Inventing Politics: A New Political Anthropology of the Hawaiian Kingdom*, (University of Hawai'i Press 2003), 161.

[35] "These Powers having received His Majesty into fraternity, it will become your duty to prepare [the King's] Government to concert in some measure with theirs." *Report of the Attorney General Read Before His Majesty, to the Hawaiian Legislature*, Wednesday, May 21st, 1845 (The Polynesian Press 1845), 5.

[36] *Id.*, 3.

[37] Kamakau, 402.

[38] Ricord "submitted at intervals portions of the succeeding code to His Majesty in cabinet council of ministers, where they have first undergone discussion and careful amendment; they have next been transferred to the Rev. William Richards, for faithful translation into the native language, after which, as from a judiciary committee, they have been reported to the legislative council for criticism, discussion, amendment, adoption or rejection." *Compilers Preface*, Statute Laws of His Majesty Kamehameha III (Government Press 1846), 6.

[39] Robert C. Lydecker, *Roster Legislatures of Hawai'i, 1841-1918* (The Hawaiian Gazette Co., Ltd. 1918), 36.

[40] Bernard Yack, "The Rationality of Hegel's Concept of Monarchy," *The American Political Science Review* 74(3) (1980): 709-720, 713.

[41] W.D. Alexander, *A Brief History of the Hawaiian People* (American Book Company 1891), 261.

[42] *Id.*

[43] *Id.*, 266.

[44] *Id.*, 267.

[45] *Id.*, 268.

[46] *Id.*, 270.

[47] *Id.*

[48] *Id.*, 277.

[49] *Id.*, 278.

[50] *Speeches of His Majesty Kamehameha IV* (Government Press 1861), 5.

[51] Lydecker, 49.

[52] *An Act to separate the office of Kuhina Nui from that of Minister of Interior Affairs*, January 6, 1855.

[53] *Compiled Laws of the Hawaiian Kingdom* (Hawaiian Gazette 1884), 199.

[54] After John Ricord left the kingdom in 1847, the office of Attorney General was not filled until 1862 with

the appointment of Charles C. Harris. During this period the District Attorneys throughout the islands performed the functions of the office.

[55] Compiled Laws, 211.

[56] On October 3, 1859, in an Extraordinary Session of the House of Nobles, Kamehameha IV received confirmation from the Nobles that his minor son, Prince Albert, was to be the successor of the Hawaiian Throne in accordance with Article twenty-five of the 1852 constitution. The young Prince died August 19, 1862, leaving the Kingdom without a successor to the throne.

[57] Lydecker, 99.

[58] *Id.*

[59] *Id.*

[60] 1864 Constitution, Article 33.

[61] 1864 Constitution, Article 20.

[62] *Reply to His Majesty's 1864 Address at the Opening of the Legislature.* Hawaiian Archives.

[63] Compiled Laws, 638.

[64] *Id.*, 639.

[65] *Id.*, 638. As a result of the illegal overthrow of the Hawaiian Kingdom government, the Board published the genealogies of Chiefs living at the time between April 20 and November 30, 1896 in the newspaper publication *Ka Maka'āinana*.

[66] Executive Documents, 574.

[67] *Id.*, 579.

[68] Compiled Laws, 8.

[69] Merze Tate, *The United States and the Hawaiian Kingdom* (Greenwood Press 1980), 91.

[70] Judd Files, Bishop Museum, MS Group Box 48.14 (July 5, 1887).

[71] 1864 Constitution, Article 80.

[72] *Id.*

[73] *Penal Code of the Hawaiian Islands*, (Government Press 1869), 8.

[74] *Id.*

[75] Executive Documents, 836.

[76] Lili'uokalani, *Hawai'i's Story by Hawai'i's Queen* (Charles E. Tuttle Co., Inc. 1964), 181.

[77] Executive Documents, 760.

[78] In the William O. Smith Collection at the Hawaiian Archives there is a near finished version of the 1887 draft with the following endorsement on the back that read: "Persons chiefly engaged in drawing up the constitution were—L.A. Thurston, Jonathan Austin, S.B. Dole, W.A. Kinney, W.O. Smith, Cecil Brown, Rev. [W.B.] Olelson, N.B. Emerson, J.A. Kennedy, [John A.] McCandless, Geo. N. Wilcox, A.S. Wilcox, H. Waterhouse, F. Wundenburg, E.G. Hitchcock, W.E. Rowell, Dr. [S.G.] Tucker, C.W. Ashford." Added to this group of individuals were Chief Justice A.F. Judd and Associate Justice Edward Preston.

[79] Executive Documents, 579.

[80] *Id.*

[81] Ralph Kuykendall, *The Hawaiian Kingdom: 1874-1893*, The Kalakaua Dynasty, vol. III (University of Hawai'i Press 1967), 407.

[82] Wodehouse to FO, no. 29, political and confidential, Aug. 30, 1887, BPRO, PO 58/220, Hawaiian Archives.

[83] Executive Documents, 579.

[84] *Id.*, 580.

[85] Kuykendall, vol. III, 448.

[86] *Id.*, 425.

[87] *Id.*, 429.

[88] *Id.*, 298.

[89] William Blackstone, *Commentaries of the Laws of England*, vol. 4 (Chicago: The University of Chicago Press 1979), 289

[90] Robert Wilcox, "Speech before the Hawaiian Legislative Assembly," *Hawaiian Kingdom* (June 10, 1890).

PART 3
United States Seizure of the Hawaiian Islands

CHAPTER 7
U.S. INTERVENTION & SETTLEMENT

L ili'uokalani's reign was fraught with political power struggles and rumors of overthrow. The 1890 McKinley
Tariff Act created an economic depression. On January 14,
1893, the Queen proclaimed her intent to reinstate the lawful
constitution in response to calls by the people and political organizations, in particular the Hui Kālai'āina (Hawaiian
Political Association).

In reaction, the leader of the 1887 revolt, Lorrin Thurston,
organized the insurgents into a Committee of Safety to plan
for the ultimate takeover of the government and to secure
annexation to the United States. The so-called Committee of
Safety sought support from U.S. Minister John L. Stevens on
January 16, 1893 to order the landing of U.S. troops to protect
the insurgents while they prepared for the annexation of the
Hawaiian Islands to the United States by a voluntary treaty of
cession.

On January 17th the group declared themselves the Provisional Government with Sanford Dole as its president. Article
31 of the Hawaiian constitution provides, "To the [Queen]
belongs the executive power." Therefore, as the constitutional
monarch, the Queen was vested with the faithful execution
of Hawaiian law, and it was her duty to ensure that certain
insurgents be apprehended by the police for committing the
crime of treason, being a violation of Chapter VI of the Penal
Code. However, under threat of war by the presence of U.S.
troops who were ordered by the U.S. diplomat Stevens to
protect the insurgents, the police force, headed by Marshall
Charles Wilson, could not apprehend the insurgents without
bloodshed between the police and U.S. troops. Later that day,
the Queen made the following assignment of executive power
under protest, called the *Lili'uokalani assignment*:

*Lorrin Thurston, a member of the
insurgency (Hawai'i Archives)*

*U.S. Minister John L. Stevens
(Hawai'i Archives)*

*Marshall Charles Wilson
(Hawai'i Archives)*

I, Lili'uokalani, by the Grace of God, and under the Constitution of the Hawaiian Kingdom, Queen, do hereby solemnly protest against any and all acts done against myself and the constitutional Government of the Hawaiian Kingdom by certain persons claiming to have established a Provisional Government of and for this Kingdom.

That I yield to the superior force of the United States of America whose Minister Plenipotentiary, His Excellency John L. Stevens, has caused United States troops to be landed at Honolulu and declared that he would support the said Provisional Government.

Now to avoid any collision of armed forces, and perhaps the loss of life, I do this under protest, and impelled by said force yield my authority until such time as the Government of the United States shall, upon facts being presented to it, undo the action of its representative and reinstate me in the authority which I claim as the constitutional sovereign of the Hawaiian Islands.

Done at Honolulu this 17th day of January, A.D. 1893.

Lili'uokalani, R.

Samuel Parker,
   Minister of Foreign Affairs.
Wm. H. Cornwell,
   Minister of Finance.
John. F. Colburn,
   Minister of the Interior.
A.P. Peterson,
   Attorney General.

In complete disregard of the Queen's protest and assignment of executive power, the Provisional Government and Secretary of State James Blaine signed a treaty on February 14, 1893 at Washington, D.C. President Benjamin Harrison submitted the treaty to the United States Senate for ratification in accordance with the U.S. Constitution. The U.S. Presidential election already had taken place in 1892, with Grover Cleveland defeating the incumbent Benjamin Harrison. After his inauguration on March 4, 1893, President Cleveland received the Queen's protest and assignment from Paul Neumann, former Hawaiian Attorney General, who, by a power of attorney, represented the Queen.

President Benjamin Harrison

President Grover Cleveland

Special Commissioner James Blount
(Hawai'i Archives)

On March 9, 1893, Cleveland withdrew the treaty from the Senate and appointed James H. Blount as Special Commissioner, a former U.S. Representative from Georgia and former Chairman of the House Committee on Foreign Affairs, as special commissioner to investigate and report his findings to Secretary of State Walter Gresham. By acccepting the Queen's temporary assignment of executive power, President Grover Cleveland bound himself and his successors in office to temporarily administer Hawaiian Kingdom law in accordance with Article 31 of the Hawaiian constitution until the executive power would be returned.

The investigation concluded that the United States diplomat and troops were directly responsible for the illegal overthrow of the Hawaiian government with the ultimate goal of transferring the Hawaiian Islands to the United States.[1] Blount reported that, "in pursuance of a prearranged plan, the Government thus established hastened off commissioners to Washington to make a treaty for the purpose of annexing the Hawaiian Islands to the United States."[2] The report also detailed United States government actions that violated international laws as well as Hawaiian territorial sovereignty.

NEGOTIATING SETTLEMENT

On October 18th 1893, U.S. Secretary of State Walter Gresham directed U.S. Minister Plenipotentiary Albert Willis to initiate negotiations with Queen Lili'uokalani:

> *On your arrival at Honolulu you will take advantage of an early opportunity to inform the Queen of...the President's sincere regret that the reprehensible conduct of the American minister and the unauthorized presence on land of a military force of the United States obliged her to surrender her sovereignty, for the time being, and rely on the justice of this Government to undo the flagrant wrong.*

You will, however, at the same time inform the Queen that, when reinstated, the President expects that she will pursue a magnanimous course by granting full amnesty to all who participated in the movement against her, including persons who are, or have been, officially or otherwise, connected with the Provisional Government, depriving them of no right or privilege which they enjoyed before the so-called revolution. All obligations created by the Provisional Government in due course of administration should be assumed.

Having secured the Queen's agreement to pursue this wise and humane policy, which it is believed you will speedily obtain, you will then advise the executive of the Provisional Government and his ministers of the President's determination of the question which their action and that of the Queen devolved upon him, and that they are expected to promptly relinquish to her constitutional authority.[3]

U.S. Minister Albert Willis

On November 13, 1893, Willis met with the Queen "who was informed that the President of the United States had important communications to make to her."[4] Willis explained the "President's sincere regret that, through the unauthorized intervention of the United States, she had been obliged to surrender her sovereignty, and his hope that, with her consent and cooperation, the wrong done to her and to her people might be redressed."[5]

The President's investigation also concluded that members of the Provisional Government and their supporters committed the crime of treason and therefore subject to the pains and penalties of treason under Hawaiian law. Willis asked the Queen: "Should you be restored to the throne, would you grant full amnesty as to life and property to all those persons who have been or who are now in the Provisional Government, or who have been instrumental in the overthrow of your government?"[6]

The Queen refused to grant amnesty and referenced Chapter VI, section 9 of the Penal Code, which states, "whoever shall commit the crime of treason shall suffer the punishment of death and all his property shall be confiscated to the Government." When asked again if she would reconsider, she responded, "these people were the cause of the revolution and the constitution of 1887. There will never be any peace while they are here. They must be sent out of the country, or punished, and their property confiscated."[7]

The government transcripts of this meeting state that the Queen called for beheading as punishment, but the Queen adamantly denied making such a statement. She later explained that beheading "is a form of punishment which has never been used in the Hawaiian

Islands, either before or since the coming of foreigners."[8] This statement, however, was leaked to newspapers in the United States for political purposes in order to portray the Queen as uncivilized and prevent restoration of the government. Despite the charge or denial of this statement, the treason statute calls for those convicted of such a high crime as treason to suffer the punishment of death.

In a follow-up dispatch to Willis, Gresham adamantly stated, "You will insist upon amnesty and recognition of obligations of the Provisional Government as essential conditions of restoration."[9] On December 3, 1893, Gresham directed Willis to continue to negotiate with the Queen, and should she "refuse assent to the written conditions you will at once inform her that the President will cease interposition in her behalf."[10] Gresham acknowledged that the President had a duty to restore the constitutional government of the Islands, but it was dependent upon an absolute agreement of the Queen to recognize the 1887 constitution, assume all administrative obligations incurred by the Provisional Government, and to grant full amnesty to those individuals instrumental in setting up or supporting the Provisional Government.

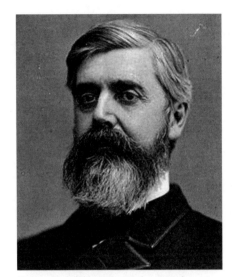

Secretary of the State Walter Gresham

He stated the "President feels that by our original interference and what followed we have incurred responsibilities to the whole Hawaiian community, and it would not be just to put one party at the mercy of the other."[11] Gresham added, "Should the Queen ask whether, if she accedes to conditions, active steps will be taken by the United States to effect her restoration, or to maintain her authority thereafter, you will say that the President can not use force without the authority of Congress."[12]

Members of the Provisional Government were not aware of the Queen's meeting with Minister Willis on November 13th, but received notice on November 24th from Lorrin Thurston who was in Washington, D.C. lobbying for annexation.[13] Four days later, Provisional Government President Sanford Dole informed the Executive Council that he had met that morning with the "military officers of the several companies in regard to the course proposed in case the U.S. forces attempt to restore the Queen. The plan being to resist till forced to yield without firing upon the U.S. troops."[14] Clearly they were determined to give the impression of being a revolutionary government, but did not want to go so far as to commit their lives to a fabricated revolution.

On December 18th 1893, the Queen's assistant, Joseph Carter notified Willis that she was willing to spare the lives of the insurgents, but not restore their property, which, "should be confiscated to the Government, and they should not be permitted to remain in the Kingdom."[15]

But later that day, the Queen sent a communication to Willis stating:

Since I had the interview with you this morning I have given the most careful and conscientious thought as to my duty, and I now of my own free will give my conclusions.

I must not feel vengeful to any of my people. If I am restored by the United States I must forget myself and remember only my dear people and my country. I must forgive and forget the past, permitting no proscription or punishment of anyone, but trusting that all will hereafter work together in peace and friendship for the good and for the glory of our beautiful and once happy land.

Asking you to bear to the President and the Government he represents a message of gratitude from me and from my people, and promising, with God's grace, to prove worthy of the confidence and friendship of your people."[16]

Queen Liliʻuokalani (Hawaiʻi Archives)

Attached to the communication was the following pledge dispatched by Willis to Gresham on December 20th 1893. An agreement between the two Heads of State had finally been made to settle the international dispute and restore the government, called the *Agreement of restoration.*[17] The Queen's declaration stated:

I, Liliʻuokalani, in recognition of the high sense of justice which has actuated the President of the United States, and desiring to put aside all feelings of personal hatred or revenge and to do what is best for all the people of these Islands, both native and foreign born, do hereby and herein solemnly declare and pledge myself that, if reinstated as the constitutional sovereign of the Hawaiian Islands, that I will immediately proclaim and declare, unconditionally and without reservation, to every person who directly or indirectly participated in the revolution of January 17, 1893, a full pardon and amnesty for their offenses, with restoration of all rights, privileges, and immunities under the constitution and the laws which have been made in pursuance thereof, and that I will forbid and prevent the adoption of any measures of proscription or punishment for what has been done in the past by those setting up or supporting the Provisional Government. I further solemnly agree to accept the restoration under the constitution existing at the time of said revolution and that I will abide by and fully execute that constitution with all the guaranties as to person and property therein contained. I furthermore solemnly pledge myself and my Government, if restored, to assume all the obligations created by the Provisional Government, in the proper course of administration, including all expenditures for military or police services, it being my purpose, if restored, to assume the Government precisely as it existed on the day when it was unlawfully overthrown.[18]

On December 18, 1893, the same day the Queen accepted the President's conditions, the President delivered a message to Congress with the results of his investigation although he was not aware that the Queen had accepted the conditions. He described the United States' action as an "act of war, committed with the participation of a diplomatic representative of the United States and without authority of Congress."[19] He acknowledged therefore the government of a peaceful and friendly people was overthrown. Cleveland further stated that a "substantial wrong has thus been done which a due regard for our national character as well as the rights of the injured people requires we should endeavor to repair,"[20] and committed to Queen Liliʻuokalani that the Hawaiian government would be restored:

> *It is a well-known rule of customary international law that third States are under a clear duty of non-intervention and non-interference in civil strife within a State. Any such interference is an unlawful act, even if, far from taking the form of military assistance to one of the parties, it is merely confined to premature recognition of the rebel government.*[21]

In his January 12, 1894 correspondence to Willis, Gresham acknowledged the Queen's acceptance of the President's offer:

> *On the 18th ultimo the President sent a special message to Congress communicating copies of Mr. Blount's reports and the instructions given to him and you. On the same day, answering a resolution of the House of Representatives, he sent copies of all correspondence since March 4, 1889, on the political affairs and relations of Hawaii, withholding, for sufficient reasons, only Mr. Stevens' No. 70 of October 8, 1892, and your No. 3 of November 16, 1893. The President therein announced that the conditions of restoration suggested by him to the Queen had not proved acceptable to her, and that since the instructions sent to you to insist upon those conditions he had not learned that the Queen was willing to assent to them. The President thereupon submitted the subject to the more extended powers and wider discretion of Congress, adding the assurance that he would be gratified to cooperate in any legitimate plan which might be devised for a solution of the problem consistent with American honor, integrity, and morality.*

> *Your reports show that on further reflection the Queen gave her unqualified assent in writing to the conditions suggested, but that the Provisional Government refuses to acquiesce in the President's decision.*

> *The matter now being in the hands of Congress the President will keep that body fully advised of the situation, and will lay before it from time to time the reports received from you, including your No. 3, heretofore withheld, and all instructions sent to you. In the meantime, while keeping the Department fully informed of the course of events, you will, until further notice, consider your special instructions upon this subject have been fully complied with.*[22]

On the following day, January 13, 1894, the President sent a follow-up message to Congress that the overthrow had been settled by negotiation and agreement with the Queen. Since the insurgents gave the impression that they would not accede to the agreements made between the Queen and President, the use of force required Congressional approval.

The Queen's declaration represented the final act of negotiation and settlement of the January 16, 1893 dispute that arose between the United States and the Hawaiian Kingdom. All that remained for the President, as the assignee of executive power, was to administer Hawaiian Kingdom law, restore the Hawaiian Kingdom government and return the executive power to the Queen, whereupon the Queen was to grant amnesty, after the criminal convictions of the insurgents, and assume administrative obligations of the provisional government.

HAWAIIAN CONSTITUTIONAL LIMITATIONS ON SETTLEMENT

Cleveland's request for a grant of general amnesty was essentially tied to the Hawaiian crime of treason and raised three questions. When did treason actually take place? Was the Queen constitutionally empowered to recognize the 1887 constitution as lawful? And was the Queen empowered under Hawaiian constitutional law to grant a pardon?[23]

Clearly, the leaders of the Provisional Government committed the crime of treason in 1887 when they forced a constitution upon King Kalākaua, the Queen's predecessor, at the point of a bayonet, and organized a new election of the legislature while the lawful legislature was serving out its term but had been out of session. The compelling purpose of the Bayonet Constitution was to offset the native voting block by placing it in the controlling hands of foreigners where "large numbers of Americans, Germans, English, and other un-naturalized foreigners were permitted to vote."[24] These elections "took place with the foreign population well armed and the troops hostile to the crown and people."[25] The insurgents of 1887 appealed to the U.S. resident Minister John Stevens to order the landing of U.S. troops in order to provide for their protection with the ultimate aim of transferring the entire territory of the Hawaiian Islands to the United States.

Further, by soliciting the intervention of the U.S. troops for their protection, these insurgents acknowledged the failure of their 1887 revolt, elevating and transforming it from a rebellion to an intervening state's violation of international law.[26] The 1864 Constitution as amended, the Civil Code, Penal Code, and the session laws of the Legislative Assembly enacted before the revolt of July 6, 1887 remained the law of the land during the revolt and continued throughout the subsequent unlawful intervention by the United States on January 16th 1893.

Hawaiian law vests the pardoning power in the executive by constitutional provision while qualifying who could administer such a power, and when it can be effected. In the United States, the President alone has the "power to grant reprieves and pardons for offenses against the United States, except in cases of impeachment."[27] In contrast, however, the Hawaiian constitution provides that the Crown, "by and with the advice of His Privy Council, has the power to grant reprieves and pardons, after conviction, for all offences, except in cases of impeachment."[28] As a constitutional monarchy, the Queen's decision to pardon, unlike the U.S. President, could only come through consultation with Her Privy Council, and the power to pardon could only be exercised after a conviction of treason.

The Hawaiian constitution also vests the law-making power solely in the Legislative Assembly comprised of the "Three Estates of this Kingdom…vested in the King, and the Legislative Assembly; which Assembly shall consist of the Nobles appointed by the King, and of the Representatives of the People, sitting together."[29]   Any change to the constitution must be first proposed in the Legislative Assembly and if later approved by the Queen "become part of the Constitution of [the] country."[30]   The *separation of powers doctrine* was fully enshrined in Hawaiian constitutional law since 1864. Hence, the 1887 Constitution was null and void since it was never submitted to the Legislative Assembly as required by the 1864 Constitution.

From a constitutional standpoint, the Queen could not recognize the 1887 Constitution without first submitting it to the Legislative Assembly convened under the lawful 1864 Constitution of the country; nor was she able to grant amnesty before or without criminal convictions of treason. Another constitutional question is whether the Queen had the power to grant a full pardon without advice from Her Privy Council. If not, a commitment by the Queen would have influenced Her Privy Council to be convened once the government was restored.

CHAPTER 8
ANNEXATION BY DECEPTION

*I*n Washington, D.C. Congress took deliberate steps to prevent the President from following through with his obligation to administer Hawaiian law and to restore the Hawaiian government, which included hearings before the Senate Foreign Relations Committee headed by Senator John Morgan, a pro-annexationist and its Chairman in 1894. These Senate hearings sought to circumvent the requirement of international law, where "a crime committed by the envoy on the territory of the receiving State must be punished by his home State."[31]   Morgan's purpose was to vindicate the illegal conduct and actions of the U.S. Legation and Naval authorities under U.S. law. Four Republicans endorsed the report with Morgan, but four Democrats submitted a minority report declaring that while they agree in exonerating the commander of the *USS Boston*, Captain Wiltse, they could not concur in exonerating "the minister of the United States, Mr. Stevens, from active officious and unbecoming participation in the events which led to the revolution in the Sandwich Islands on the 14th, 16th, and 17th of January, 1893."[32]

By contradicting Blount's investigation, Morgan intended, as a matter of congressional action, to bar the President from restoring the government as was previously agreed upon with the Queen because there was fervor of annexation among many members of Congress. On February 7, 1894, the House of Representatives passed the following resolution:

> Resolved *First. That it is the sense of this House that the action of the United States minister in employing United States naval forces and illegally aiding in overthrowing the constitutional Government of the Hawaiian Islands in January, 1893, and in setting up in its place a Provisional Government not republican in form and in opposition to the will of a majority of the people, was contrary to the traditions of our Republic and the spirit of our Constitution, and should be and is condemned.*

> *Second. That we heartily approve the principle announced by the President of the United States that interference with the domestic affairs of an independent nation is contrary to the spirit of American institutions. And it is further the sense of this House that the annexation of the Hawaiian Islands to our country, or the assumption of a protectorate over them by our Government, is uncalled for and inexpedient; that the people of that country should have had absolute freedom and independence in pursuing their own line of policy, and that foreign intervention in the political affairs of the islands will not be regarded with indifference by the Government of the United States.*

On May 31st 1894, the U.S. Senate passed a similar resolution warning other countries to not intervene in Hawaiian affairs.

> *Resolved, That of right-it-belongs wholly to the people of the Hawaiian Islands to establish and maintain their own form of Government and domestic policy; that the United States ought in no wise to interfere therewith, and that any intervention in the political affairs of these islands by any other Government will be regarded as an act unfriendly to the United States.*

Cleveland's failure to fulfill his obligation of the agreement allowed the insurgents to gain strength, and on July 4, 1894, they renamed themselves the Republic of Hawai'i. For the next three years they maintained their authority with hired mercenaries and force of arms. They arrested and imprisoned Hawaiian nationals who resisted their authority with the threat of execution and tried the Queen on fabricated evidence to coerce her into abdicating the throne.[33]

President William McKinley

On June 16, 1897, Cleveland's successor William McKinley entered into a second treaty of cession with the same insurgents who presented themselves as the Republic of Hawai'i. This second attempt to acquire the Hawaiian Islands by treaty would "be taken up immediately upon the convening of Congress next December."[34]

Queen Lili'uokalani was in the United States at the time of the signing of the treaty and protested the second annexation attempt. While in Washington, D.C., the Queen filed a diplomatic protest with the United States Department of State on June 17th 1897:

I, Lili'uokalani of Hawai'i, by the will of God named heir apparent on the tenth day of April, A.D. 1877, and by the grace of God Queen of the Hawaiian Islands on the seventeenth day of January, A.D. 1893, do hereby protest against the ratification of a certain treaty, which, so I am informed, has been signed at Washington by Messrs. Hatch, Thurston, and Kinney, purporting to cede those Islands to the territory and dominion of the United States. I declare such a treaty to be an act of wrong toward the native and part-native people of Hawai'i, an invasion of the rights of the ruling chiefs, in violation of international rights both toward my people and toward friendly nations with whom they have made treaties, the perpetuation of the fraud whereby the constitutional government was overthrown, and, finally, an act of gross injustice to me.

BECAUSE *the official protests made by me on the seventeenth day of January, 1893, to the so-called Provisional Government was signed by me, and received by said government with the assurance that the case was referred to the United States of America for arbitration.*

BECAUSE *that protest and my communications to the United States Government immediately thereafter expressly declare that I yielded my authority to the forces of the United States in order to avoid bloodshed, and because I recognized the futility of a conflict with so formidable a power.*

BECAUSE *the President of the United States, the Secretary of State, and an envoy commissioned by them reported in official documents that my government was unlawfully coerced by the forces, diplomatic and naval, of the United States; that I was at the date of their investigations the constitutional ruler of my people.*

BECAUSE *neither the above-named commission nor the government which sends it has ever received any such authority from the registered voters of Hawai'i, but derives its assumed powers from the so-called committee of public safety, organized on or about the seventeenth day of January, 1893, said committee being composed largely of persons claiming American citizenship, and not one single Hawaiian was a member thereof, or in any way participated in the demonstration leading to its existence.*

BECAUSE *my people, about forty thousand in number, have in no way been consulted by those, three thousand in number, who claim the right to destroy the independence of Hawai'i. My people constitute four-fifths of the legally qualified voters of Hawai'i, and excluding those imported for the demands of labor, about the same proportion of the inhabitants.*

BECAUSE *said treaty ignores, not only the civic rights of my people, but, further, the hereditary property of their chiefs. Of the 4,000,000 acres composing the territory said treaty offers to annex, 1,000,000 or 915,000 acres has in no way been heretofore recognized as other than the private property of the constitutional monarch, subject to a control in no way differing from other items of a private estate.*

BECAUSE *it is proposed by said treaty to confiscate said property, technically called the crown lands, those legally entitled thereto, either now or in succession, receiving no consideration whatever for estates, their title to which has been always undisputed, and which is legitimately in my name at this date.*

BECAUSE *said treaty ignores, not only all professions of perpetual amity and good faith made by the United States in former treaties with the sovereigns representing the Hawaiian people, but all treaties made by those sovereigns with other and friendly powers, and it is thereby in violation of international law.*

BECAUSE, *by treating with the parties claiming at this time the right to cede said territory of Hawai'i, the Government of the United States receives such territory from the hands of those whom its own magistrates (legally elected by the people of the United States, and in office in 1893) pronounced fraudulently in power and unconstitutionally ruling Hawai'i.*

THEREFORE I, Lili'uokalani of Hawai'i, *do hereby call upon the President of that nation, to whom alone I yielded my property and my authority, to withdraw said treaty (ceding said Islands) from further consideration. I ask the honorable Senate of the United States to decline to ratify said treaty, and I implore the people of this great and good nation, from whom my ancestors learned the Christian religion, to sustain their representatives in such acts of justice and equity as may be in accord with the principles of their fathers, and to the Almighty Ruler of the universe, to him who judgeth righteously, I commit my cause.*

Done at Washington, District of Columbia, United States of America, this seventeenth day of June, in the year eighteen hundred and ninety-seven.

[signed] *Lili'uokalani*

[signed] *Joseph Heleluhe   )*
[signed] *Wakeki Heleluhe   ) Witness to signature*
[signed] *Julius A. Palmer   )* [35]

Hawaiian political organizations, including the Men and Women's Hawaiian Patriotic League (Hui Aloha ʻĀina), and the Hawaiian Political Association (Hui Kālaiʻāina) filed additional protests with the Department of State in Washington, D.C.[36] In addition, a petition with 21,269 signatures of Hawaiian subjects and resident aliens protesting annexation was filed with the Senate when it convened in December 1897.[37] The Senate was unable to garner enough votes to ratify the treaty, but events quickly changed as the Spanish-American war loomed.

Signature Petition, Hawaiian Patriotic League (Hui Aloha ʻĀina)

HAWAIIAN NEUTRALITY VIOLATED DURING SPANISH-AMERICAN WAR

On April 25, 1898, Congress declared war on Spain. On the following day, President McKinley issued a proclamation that stated, "It being desirable that such war should be conducted upon principles in harmony with the present views of nations and sanctioned by their recent practice."[38]

Battles were fought in the Spanish colonies of Puerto Rico and Cuba, as well as the Spanish colonies of the Philippines and Guam. After Commodore George Dewey defeated the Spanish fleet in the Philippines on May 1, 1898, the *U.S.S. Charleston*, a protected cruiser, was re-commissioned on May 5th and ordered to lead a convoy of 2,500 troops to reinforce Dewey in the Philippines and Guam. These troops traveled on the transport ships of the *City of Peking*, the *City of Sydney* and the *Australia*.

In a deliberate violation of Hawaiian neutrality during the war, this convoy sailed on May 21st to the Hawaiian Islands for re-coaling. The ships arrived in Honolulu on June 1st, and took on 1,943 tons of coal before it left the islands on June 4th.[39] A second convoy of troops bound for the Philippines on the transport ships the *China, Zelandia, Colon,* and the *Senator* arrived in Honolulu on June 23rd and took on 1,667 tons of coal.[40] During this time, international law regulated the supply of coal for belligerent ships entering a neutral port.

U.S. Troops Arriving in Honolulu Harbor During the Spanish-American War (Hawai'i Archives)

When it became apparent that the Republic of Hawai'i, which was installed by the U.S. since 1893, had welcomed the U.S. naval convoys and assisted in re-coaling their ships, Spanish Vice-Counsel H. Renjes in Honolulu lodged a formal protest on June 1, 1898:

> *In my capacity as Vice Consul for Spain, I have the honor today to enter a formal protest with the Hawaiian Government against the constant violations of Neutrality in this harbor, while actual war exists between Spain and the United States of America.*[41]

In a dispatch dated June 8th, Minister Harold Sewall, the U.S. Diplomat in Honolulu, notified Secretary of State William R. Day of Renjes' protest.[42]

An article published in the *American Historical Review*, Thomas Andrew Bailey, an American historian, wrote: "although the United States had given formal notice of the existence of war to the other powers, in order that they might proclaim neutrality, and was jealously watching their behavior, she was flagrantly violating the neutrality of Hawai'i."[43] He also stated:

The position of the United States was all the more reprehensible in that she was compelling a weak nation to violate the international law that had to a large degree been formulated by her own stand on the Alabama *claims. Furthermore, in line with the precedent established by the Geneva award, Hawai'i would be liable for every cent of damage caused by her dereliction as a neutral, and for the United States to force her into this position was cowardly and ungrateful. At the end of the war, Spain or cooperating power would doubtless occupy Hawai'i, indefinitely if not permanently, to insure payment of damages, with the consequent jeopardizing of the defenses of the Pacific Coast.*[44]

The *Alabama claims* was an arbitration case between Great Britain and the United States that convened in Geneva, Switzerland, from 1871-1872. The United States alleged that Great Britain violated its neutrality by allowing Confederate warships to be built in Liverpool that wreaked havoc on Union merchant ships during the Civil War. The arbitration tribunal agreed and awarded the United States $15.5 million dollars in damages, also known as the Geneva award.

U.S. Troops Posing With Insurgents Sanford Dole (center) and W.O. Smith (left) (Hawai'i Archives)

The United States violated Hawaiian neutrality during the Spanish-American war through the puppet government it created in 1893 and then calling it the Republic of Hawai'i since 1894. According to Krystyna Marek, an expert in international law:

Puppet governments are organs of the occupant and, as such form part of his legal order. The agreements concluded by them with the occupant are not genuine international agreements, however correct in form; failing a genuine contracting party, such agreements are merely decrees of the occupant disguised as agreements which the occupant in fact concludes with himself. Their measures and laws are those of the occupant.[45]

JUSTIFYING CONGRESSIONAL ACTION TO ANNEX

After the defeat of the Spanish Pacific Squadron in the Philippines, U.S. Congressman Francis Newlands (D-Nevada), submitted House Resolution 259 annexing the Hawaiian Islands (also known as the Newlands Resolution), to the House Committee on Foreign Affairs on May 4, 1898. Six days later, hearings were held on the Newlands Resolution, and U.S. Naval Captain Alfred Mahan's testimony explained the military significance of the Hawaiian Islands to the United States:

It is obvious that if we do not hold the islands ourselves we cannot expect the neutrals in the war to prevent the other belligerent from occupying them; nor can the inhabitants themselves prevent such occupation. The commercial value is not great enough to provoke neutral interposition. In short, in war we should need a larger Navy to defend the Pacific coast, because we should have not only to defend our own coast, but to prevent, by naval force, an enemy from occupying the islands; whereas, if we preoccupied them, fortifications could preserve them to us. In my opinion it is not practicable for any trans-Pacific country to invade our Pacific coast without occupying Hawai'i as a base[46]

Captain Alfred Mahan

General John Schofield of the Army also provided testimony to the committee justifying the seizure of the Islands:

We got a preemption title to those islands through the volunteer action of our American missionaries who went there and civilized and Christianized those people and established a Government that has no parallel in the history of the world, considering its age, and we made a preemption which nobody in the world thinks of disputing, provided we perfect our title. If we do not perfect it in due time, we have lost those islands. Anybody else can come in and undertake to get them. So it seems to me the time is now ripe when this Government should do that which has been in contemplation from the beginning as a necessary consequence of the first action of our people in going there and settling those islands and establishing a good Government and education and the action of our Government from that time forward on every suitable occasion in claiming the right of American influence over those islands, absolutely excluding any other foreign power from any interference.[47]

General John Schofield

On May 17, 1898, U.S. Congressman Robert Hitt (R-Illinois) reported the Newlands Resolution out of the House Committee on Foreign Affairs, and entered the House of Representatives for debate. There was strong opposition to the resolution on constitutional grounds because cessions can only take place by treaty, which is a bilateral agreement between two sovereign States. A joint resolution of Congress is not only a unilateral act, but also legislation that international law imposes "strict territorial limits on national assertions of legislative jurisdiction.[48] Therefore, in order to give the impression of conformity to cessions recognizable under international law, the Newlands Resolution included the text of the failed treaty. Congressman Thomas H. Ball (D-Texas) stated:

> *The annexation of Hawai'i by joint resolution is unconstitutional, unnecessary, and unwise. If the first proposition be true, sworn to support the Constitution, we should inquire no further. I challenge not the advocates of Hawaiian annexation, but those who advocate annexation in the form now presented, to show warrant or authority in our organic law for such acquisition of territory. To do so will be not only to subvert the supreme law of the land but to strike down every precedent in our history. ... Why, sir, the very presence of this measure here is the result of a deliberate attempt to do unlawfully that which can not be done lawfully.[49]*

Despite the constitutional objections, the House passed the resolution on June 15th and then moved to the Senate.[50]   However, it became clear before the resolution reached the Senate on June 16th, the Senators had already been discussing annexation by resolution on May 31st.[51] During a debate on the Revenue Bill for funding the war, the Senate went into secret executive session to discuss annexation. Senator David Turpie (D-Indiana) made a motion to have the Senate enter into secret session and according to Senate rule thirty-five, the galleries were ordered cleared and the doors closed to the public. The transcripts of the Senate's secret session, however, would later prove to be important.[52]

Senator Stephen White

From June 16 to July 6, 1898, the annexation resolution was in the Senate. On June 22nd, the New York Times reported Senator Stephen White (D-California) on Senate floor "demanded to know what cession had been made, and what lawyer in the Senate would state that there had been a cession. He maintained there had been no cession, as there could not have been without the concurrence of both parties."[53] Senator Augustus Bacon (D-Georgia) stated:

> *That a joint resolution for the annexation of foreign territory was necessarily and essentially the subject matter of a treaty, and that it could not be accomplished legally and constitutionally by a statute or joint resolution. If Hawai'i was to be annexed, it ought certainly to be annexed by a constitutional method; and if by a constitutional method it can not be annexed, no Senator ought to desire its an-*

Senator Augustus Bacon

nexation sufficiently to induce him to give his support to an unconstitutional measure.

…Now, a statute is this: A Statute is a rule of conduct laid down by the legislative department, which has its effect upon all of those within the jurisdiction. In other words, a statute passed by the Congress of the United States is obligatory upon every person who is a citizen of the United States or a resident therein. A statute can not go outside the jurisdiction of the United States and be binding upon the subjects of another power. It takes the consent of the subjects of the other power, speaking or giving their consent through their duly authorized government, to be bound by a certain thing which is enacted in this country; and therein comes the necessity for a treaty.

What is it that the House of Representatives has done? …The friends of annexation, seeing that it was impossible to make the treaty in the manner pointed out by the Constitution, attempted then to nullify the provision in the Constitution by putting that treaty in the form of a statute, and here we have embodied the provisions of the treaty in the joint resolution which comes to us from the House.[54]

Proponents of annexation relied on article IV, section 3 of the U.S. Constitution, which provides that "New States may be admitted by the Congress into this Union." Supporters in both the House and Senate relied on the precedent set by the 28th Congress when it annexed Texas by joint resolution on March 1, 1845.[55] Opponents argued that the precedent was misplaced because Texas was admitted as a State, whereas Hawai'i was not being annexed as a State, but as a territory. Supporters of annexation, like Senator Elkin (R-West Virginia), reasoned that if Congress could annex a State, it could annex a territory.[56] Whatever the argument made, Congressional laws have no force beyond the borders of the United States and it wasn't the joint resolution that annexed Texas. Rather, it was the 1848 Treaty of Guadalupe-Hidalgo that ended the Mexican-American war that effectively ceded Mexican territory north of the Rio Grande River to the United States, which included Texas. In fact, the joint resolution started the war in the first place.

Nevertheless, on July 6, 1898, the United States Congress passed the joint resolution purportedly annexing Hawaiian territory. President McKinley signed the resolution on the following day, which proclaimed that the cession of the Hawaiian Islands had been "accepted, ratified, and confirmed."[57] Annexation is the act of attaching or joining, while cession is to convey or grant by agreement. In other words, annexation does not precede cession, but is the result of cession or grant by another sovereign State.

Like a carefully rehearsed play, the annexation ceremony of August 12, 1898, by a minority few was scripted to appear to abide by international law. On a stage in front of the 'Iolani Palace in Honolulu, the following exchange took place between Harold Sewell, U.S. Minister to Hawai'i, and Sanford Dole, starring as the President of the so-called Republic of Hawai'i.

Mr. SEWELL: "Mr. President, I present to you a certified copy of a joint resolution of the Congress of the United States, approved by the President on July 7th, 1898, entitled "Joint Resolution to provide for annexing the Hawaiian Islands to the United States. This joint resolution accepts, ratifies and confirms, on the part of the United States, the cession formally consented to and approved by the Republic of Hawai'i."

Mr. DOLE: A treaty of political union having been made, and the cession formally consented to and approved by the Republic of Hawai'i, having been accepted by the United States of America, I now, in the interest of the Hawaiian body politic, and with full confidence in the honor, justice and friendship of the American people, yield up to you as the representative of the Government of the United States, the sovereignty and public property of the Hawaiian Islands.

Mr. SEWELL: In the name of the United States, I accept the transfer of the sovereignty and property of the Hawaiian Government.[58]

Many government officials and constitutional scholars were unable to explain how a joint resolution could have extra-territorial force in annexing the Hawaiian Islands because "American courts, commentators, and other authorities understood international law as imposing strict territorial limits on national assertions of legislative jurisdiction."[59]

The U.S. Supreme Court explained, "that the legislation of every country is territorial,"[60] and that the "laws of no nation can justly extend beyond its own territory" for it would be "at variance with the independence and sovereignty of foreign nations."[61]

Sanford Dole, head of the insurgency (left) and U.S. Minister Harold Sewell (right) (Hawai'i Archives)

The Court also stated, "however general and comprehensive the phrases used in our municipal laws may be, they must always be restricted in construction, to places and persons, upon whom the legislature have authority and jurisdiction."[62]

Acting Assistant U.S. Attorney General, Douglas W. Kmiec, concluded in 1988 that it was "unclear which constitutional power Congress exercised when it acquired Hawai'i by joint resolution."[63] And constitutional scholar and political scientist Westel Willoughby summed it all up in this statement:

The constitutionality of the annexation of Hawai'i, by a simple legislative act, was strenuously contested at the time both in Congress and by the press. The right to annex by treaty was not denied, but it was denied that this might be done by a simple legislative act....Only by means of treaties, it was asserted, can the relations between States be governed, for a legislative act is necessarily without extraterritorial force—confined in its operation to the territory of the State by whose legislature it is enacted.[64]

CHAPTER 9
U.S. SENATE SECRET SESSION TO SEIZE HAWAI'I

The intent and purpose of the 1898 joint resolution of annexation would not be uncovered until January 1969, after a historian noted there were gaps in the Congressional records. The transcripts of the Senate's secret session, 70 years earlier, were made public after the Senate passed a resolution authorizing the U.S. National Archives to open the records. The Associated Press in Washington, D.C., reported that "the secrecy was clamped on during a debate over whether to seize the Hawaiian Islands—called the Sandwich Islands then—or merely developing leased areas of Pearl Harbor to reinforce the U.S. fleet at Manila Bay."[65]

These transcripts divulged that the true intent of the Senate was to have the joint resolution serve merely as Congressional consent for the President to utilize his war powers in the occupation and seizure of the Hawaiian Islands as a matter of military necessity.

First U.S. Military Base, Camp McKinley, 1898 (Hawai'i Archives)

On May 31, 1898, just a few weeks after the defeat of the Spanish fleet in Manila Bay in the Philippines, and with the knowledge that the McKinley Administration had deliberately violated Hawaiian neutrality, the Senate entered into its secret session. On this day, Senator Henry Cabot Lodge (R-Massachusetts) argued that the "Administration was compelled to violate the neutrality of those islands, that protests from foreign representatives had already been received and complications with other powers were threatened, that the annexation or some action in regard to those islands had become a military necessity."[66]

DISTINGUISHING MILITARY GOVERNMENT FROM MARTIAL LAW

At the time of the Spanish-American War, leading legal authority on U.S. military occupations included the seminal case ex parte Milligan and William Birkhimer's publication "Military Government and Martial Law." In 1892, Birkhimer, an Army officer at the time, wrote the first of three editions that distinguished between military government and martial law—the "former is exercised over enemy territory; the latter over loyal territory of the State enforcing it."[67] Birkhimer sought to expound on what Chief Justice Salmon Chase noted in his dissenting opinion in *ex parte Milligan* regarding military government and martial law that exist under U.S. law.[68] According to Birkhimer, the distinction is important whereby "military government is…placed within the domain of international law, while martial law is within the cognizance of municipal law."[69]

From a careful review of the transcripts of the secret session, it seems likely that the Senators, particularly Senator John Morgan (D-Alabama), were not only familiar with Birkhimer's publication, but also with Chief Justice Chase's statement regarding the establishment of a military government on foreign soil. Chase stated that military government is established "under the direction of the President, with the express or implied sanction of Congress."[70] Relevant passages from Birkhimer on this subject include:

> …*The instituting military government in any country by the commander of a foreign army there is not only a belligerent right, but often a duty. It is incidental to the state of war, and appertains to the law of nations.*

> …*The commander of the invading, occupying, or conquering army rules the country with supreme power, limited only by international law, and the orders of his government.*

> …*As commander-in-chief the President is authorized to direct the movements of the naval and military forces, and to employ them in the manner he may deem most effectual to harass, conquer, and subdue the enemy. He may invade the hostile country and subject it to the sovereignty and authority of the United States.*

Senator Morgan, an ardent proponent of annexation, knew first hand the limitation of exercising sovereignty beyond a State's borders as a member of the Senate Foreign Relations Committee in 1884. In 1882, the American schooner *Daylight* was anchored outside the Mexican harbor of Tampico when a Mexican gunship collided with the schooner during a storm.[71] The Mexican authorities took the position that any claim for damages by the owners of the schooner should be prosecuted through Mexican tribunals and not through diplomatic channels, but the United States emphatically denied this claim.[72] U.S. Secretary of State Frederick Frelinghuysen explained to Senator Morgan in a letter that, it is the "uniform declaration of writers on public law [that] in an international point of view, either the thing or the person made the subject of jurisdiction must be within the territory, for no sovereignty can extend its process beyond its own territorial limits."[73]

ANNEXATION JUSTIFIED AS A WAR NECESSITY

As evidenced in Morgan's exchange with Senator William Allen (P-Nebraska) in the secret session, the joint resolution was never intended to have any extra-territorial force, but was simply an "enabler" for the President to occupy the Hawaiian Islands. In other words, it was not a matter of U.S. constitutional law, but merely served as an "express sanction" of the Congress to support the President as their commander-in-chief in the war against Spain. Morgan, who was fully aware of the two failed attempts to annex Hawai'i by a treaty of cession, attempted to apply a perverse reasoning of military jurisdiction over the Hawaiian Islands. The term annexation, as used in these transcripts, was not in the context of affixing or bringing together two separate territories. Rather, it was a matter of taking and claiming Hawaiian territory for oneself without right, but justified under the principle of military necessity.

Senator William Allen

Senator John Morgan

Mr. ALLEN. I do not desire to interrupt the Senator needlessly, but I want to understand his position. I infer the Senator means that Congress shall legislate and establish a civil government over territory before it is conquered and that legislation may be carried into execution when the country is reduced by force of our arms?

Mr. MORGAN. What I mean is, the President having no prerogative powers, but deriving his powers from the law, that Congress shall enact a law to enable him to do it, and not leave it to his unbridled will and judgment.

Mr. ALLEN. Would it not be just as wise, then, to provide a code of laws for the government of a neutral territory in anticipation that within five or six months we might declare war against that power and reduce its territory?

Mr. MORGAN. I am not discussing the wisdom of that.

Mr. ALLEN. Would it not be exceptional because we have never before had a foreign war like this, or anything approximating to it. All I am contending for at this time, and all I intend to contend for at any time, is that the President of the United States shall have the powers conferred upon him by Congress full and ample, but that he shall understand that they come from Congress and do not come from his prerogative, or whatever his powers may be merely as the fighting agent of the United States, the Commander-in-Chief of the Army and Navy of the United States.

Mr. ALLEN. That would arise from his constitutional powers as Commander-in-Chief of the Army and the Navy.

Mr. MORGAN. No; his constitutional powers as Commander-in-Chief of the Army and the Navy are not defined in that instrument. When he is in foreign countries he draws his powers from the laws of nations, but when he is at home fighting rebels or Indians, or the like of that, he draws them from the laws of the United States, for the enabling power comes from Congress, and without it he cannot turn a wheel.[74]

These transcripts are as integral to the Newlands Resolution as if it were written in the resolution itself. According to Justice Swayne of the U.S. Supreme Court in 1874, "The intention of the lawmaker is the law."[75] The intent of the Senate was to utilize the President's war powers and not congressional authority to annex. Ironically, it was the U.S. Supreme Court in *Territory of Hawai'i v. Mankichi* that underscored this principle and, in particular, referenced Swayne's statement when the court was faced with the question of whether or not the Newlands Resolution extended the U.S. Constitution over the Hawaiian Islands.[76] Unfortunately, due to the injunction of secrecy imposed by the Senate in 1898 regarding these transcripts,

1898 Cartoon of a Shotgun Wedding— Puck Magazine (Hawai'i Archives)

the Supreme Court had no access to these records when it arrived at its decision in 1903. The Supreme Court did, however, create a legal fiction to be used as a qualifying source for the Newlands resolution's extra-territorial effect.

According to L.L. Fuller, a legal fiction "may sometimes mean simply a false statement having a certain utility, whether it was believed by its author or not," and "an expedient but false assumption."[77] The utility of *Mankichi* would later prove useful when questions arose regarding the annexation of territory by legislative action.[78] Because Congressional legislation could neither annex Hawaiian territory, nor affect Hawaiian sovereignty, there is strong legal basis to believe that Hawai'i remained a sovereign State under international law when the U.S. unilaterally seized the Hawaiian Islands by way of a joint resolution. According to Professor Eyal Benvenisti, this legal basis stems from "the principle of inalienable sovereignty over a territory," which "spring the constraints that international law imposes upon the occupant."[79]

KEY CONCEPTS

International Law   Duty of Non-intervention   Treaty
Ratification   Cession   Annexation
Congressional Authority   Joint Resolution

FURTHER CONSIDERATION

1. Most people assume that the overthrow of the Hawaiian Kingdom government was not settled, but history shows otherwise. Break out into groups and discuss what were the circumstances of the settlement and why is it that people today didn't know this.

2. Under the U.S. Constitution there are three branches of government—Legislative (Congress), Executive (President), and Judicial (Courts). Discuss the functions of each branch and their limitations regarding the overthrow of the Hawaiian Kingdom government. Which of the three branches can exercise its authority beyond the territory of the United States?

3. Is there a difference between the terms cession and annexation? Explain.

[1] United States House of Representatives, 53rd Congress, Executive Documents on Affairs in Hawai'i: 1894-95, (Government Printing Office 1895), 567, [hereafter Executive Documents]. Reprinted at *Hawaiian Journal of Law & Politics* 1 (Summer 2004): 136.

[2] *Id.,* Executive Documents, 587.

[3] *Id.*, 1190.

[4] *Id.*, 1242.

[5] *Id.*

[6] *Id.*

[7] *Id.*

[8] Lili'uokalani, *Hawai'i's Story by Hawai'i's Queen* (Charles E. Tuttle Co., Inc. 1964), 247.

[9] Executive Documents, 1191.

[10] *Id.*

[11] *Id.*

[12] *Id.*, 1192.

[13] "Executive Council Minutes," *Republic of Hawai'i* (November 24, 1893), 111.

[14] *Id.* (November 28, 1893), 115.

[15] Executive Documents, 1267.

[16] *Id.*, 1269.

[17] David Keanu Sai, "A Slippery Path Towards Hawaiian Indigeneity," 10 *Journal of Law and Social Challenges* (Fall 2008) 68-133.

[18] *Id.*

[19] Executive Documents, *456.*

[20] *Id.*

[21] Krystyna Marek, *Identity and Continuity of States in Public International Law*, 2nd ed., (Librairie Droz 1968), 64.

[22] Executive Documents, 1283-1284.

[23] Sai, Slippery Path, 121-125.

[24] Executive Documents, 579.

[25] *Id.*

[26] United States doctrine at the time considered rebellions to be successful when the insurgents are (1) in complete control of all governmental machinery, (2) there exists no organized resistance, and (3) acquiescence of the people. See also John Basset Moore, *Digest of International Law*, Vol. I (Government Printing Office 1906), 139.

[27] U.S. Constitution (1787), Article II, §2.

[28] Hawaiian Constitution (1864), Article 27.

[29] *Id.*, Article 45.

[30] *Id.*, Article 80.

[31] Lassa Oppenheim, *International Law*, 3rd ed. (Longmans, Green & Co. 1920), 252.

[32] Senate Report 227 (February 26, 1894), *Reports of Committee on Foreign Relations 1789-1901* Volume 6, 53rd Congress, 363.

[33] Two days before the Queen was arrested on charges of misprision of treason, Sanford Dole, President of the so-called Republic of Hawai'i, admitted in an executive meeting on January 14, 1894, that "there was no legal evidence of the complicity of the ex-queen to cause her arrest…" *Minutes of the Executive Council of the Republic of Hawai'i*, 159 (Hawai'i Archives).

[34] "Hawaiian Treaty to Wait—Senator Morgan Suggests that It Be Taken Up at This Session Without Result." *The New York Times*, 3 (July 25, 1897).

[35] Lili'uokalani, 354. 1897 Protest reprinted at Hawaiian Journal of Law & Politics 1 (Summer 2004): 227.

[36] Tom Coffman, *Nation Within: The Story of America's Annexation of the Nation of Hawai'i* (Tom Coffman/Epicenter 1999), 268.

[37] Noenoe Silva, *Aloha Betrayed: Native Hawaiian Resistance to American Colonialism* (Duke University Press 2004), 145-159. See also Coffman, 273-287.

[38] 30 U.S. Stat. 1770.

[39] U.S. Minister to Hawai'i Harold Sewall to U.S. Secretary of State William R. Day, No. 167, (June 4, 1898), Hawai'i Archives.

[40] *Id.*, No. 175 (27 June 1898).

[41] Sewall to Day, No. 168 (8 June 1898).

[42] *Id.*

[43] T.A. Bailey, "The United States and Hawai'i During the Spanish-American War," *The American Historical Review* 36(3) (April 1931): 552-560, 557.

[44] *Id.*

[45] Marek, 114.

[46] 31 Cong. Record, 5771 (1898).

[47] *Id.*

[48] Gary Born, *International Civil Litigation in United States Courts*, 3rd ed., (Kluwer Law International 1996), 493.

[49] 31 Cong. Record, 5975 (1898).

[50] *Id.*, 6019.

[51] Associated Press, "Secret Debate on U.S. Seizure of Hawai'i Revealed," Honolulu Star-Bulletin, A1 (February 1, 1969).

[52] *Id.*

[53] "Objections to Hawaii—Opponents to Annexation Have the Floor in the Senate and Present Arguments," *New York Times* (June 21, 1898).

[54] 31 Cong. Record, 6148, 6150 (1898).

[55] Congressional Globe, 28th Congress, 2nd Session (1845), 372.

[56] 31 Cong. Record, 6149 (1898).

[57] 30 U.S. Stat. 750.

[58] Lorrin A. Thurston, *The Fundamental Law of Hawai'i* (The Hawaiian Gazette Co., Ltd. 1904), 253.

[59] Born, 493.

[60] *Rose v. Himely*, 8 U.S. 241, 279 (1807).

[61] *The Apollon*, 22 U.S. 362, 370 (1824).

[62] *Id.*

[63] Douglas Kmiec, "Legal Issues Raised by Proposed Presidential Proclamation To Extend the Territorial Sea," *Opinions of the Office of Legal Counsel of the U.S. Department of Justice* 12 (1988): 238-263, 262.

[64] Westel Willoughby, The Constitutional Law of the United States, 2nd ed., (Baker, Voorhis 1929), 427.

[65] Associated Press, A1.

[66] "Transcript of the Senate Secret Session on Seizure of the Hawaiian Islands, May 31, 1898," *Hawaiian Journal of Law & Politics* 1 (Summer 2004): 280.

[67] William E. Birkhimer, *Military Government and Martial Law* (James J. Chapman 1892), 1.

[68] Associated Press, A1.

[69] Birkhimer, 1.

[70] *Ex parte Milligan*, 142.

[71] John Basset Moore, *Digest of International Law*, vol. 6, (U.S. Government Printing Office 1906), 679.

[72] *Id.*

[73] Letter concerning the Schooner Daylight from Secretary of State Frelinghuysen to Mr. Morgan, dated May 17, 1884, reprinted in *Foreign Relations of the United States* 358 (1885). It was later determined by a General Claims Commission (United States and Mexico) convened to hear the *Daylight Case*, docket no. 353 (1927), that the collision did occur "in Mexican waters and Mexican law is applicable. The law in force in Mexico at the time of the collision contained no presumption in favor of ships at anchor or in favor of sailing ships in collision with steamers." "Judicial Decisions Involving Questions of International Law," *The American Journal of International Law*, 21 (4) (Oct., 1927): 777-811, 791.

[74] Transcript of the Senate Secret Session, 269.

[75] *Smythe v. Fiske*, 90 U.S. (23 Wall.) 374, 380 (1874).

[76] *Territory of Hawai'i v. Mankichi*, 190 U.S. 197, 212 (1903).

[77] L.L. Fuller, "Legal Fictions," *Illinois Law Review* 25 (Dec. 1930): 363-399, 369.

[78] Christopher Schroeder, "Validity of Congressional-Executive Agreements that Substantially Modify the United States' obligations Under an Existing Treaty," *Opinions of the Office of Legal Counsel of the U.S. Department of Justice* 20 (1996): 389-401, 398, note 19.

[79] Eyal Benvenisti, *The International Law of Occupation* (Princeton University Press 1993), 5.

PART 4

Prolonged Occupation of the Hawaiian Kingdom

CHAPTER 10
OCCUPATION

Since 1900, the U.S. migration to Hawai'i, predominantly by U.S. military personnel and their families, has grown exponentially. Hawai'i has played a role in nearly every major U.S. armed conflict because of this military presence and the island's strategic location. In 1911, U.S. Army Commander Brigadier General Macomb, District of Hawai'i, stated, "O'ahu is to be encircled with a ring of steel, with mortar batteries at Diamond Head, big guns at Waikīkī and Pearl Harbor, and a series of redoubts from Koko Head around the island to Wai'anae."[1]

In 1924, U.S. Territorial Governor Wallace Rider Farrington further stated, "Every day is national defense in Hawai'i."[2] Since 1947, Hawai'i has been the headquarters for the single largest combined U.S. military presence in the world, the U.S. Pacific Command.[3]

Brigadier General Macomb

Wallace Rider Farrington
(Hawai'i Archives)

One of the fundamental duties of an occupier is to maintain the *status quo ante* for the national population of the occupied State. This principle applies to those who possess the nationality or political status of the Hawaiian Kingdom. Thus the U.S. is precluded from affecting the national population through mass migration and/or birth of U.S. citizens within Hawaiian territory.

Hawaiian law recognizes three ways of acquiring citizenship: by application to the Minister of the Interior for naturalization; citizenship by birth on Hawaiian territory (*jus soli*); and citizenship acquired by descent of Hawaiian subjects for children born abroad.[4] U.S. citizens, as citizens of a foreign government, are prevented from exercising the first two means of acquiring Hawaiian citizenship. One scholar explains that, "the nationality of the inhabitants of occupied areas does not ordinarily change through the mere fact that temporary rule of a foreign government has been instituted, inasmuch as military occupation does not confer *de jure* sovereignty upon an occupant. Thus under the laws of most countries, children born in territory under enemy occupation possess the nationality of their parents, that is, that of the legitimate sovereign of the occupied area."[5]

Therefore, any individual today who is a direct descendent of a person who lawfully acquired Hawaiian citizenship prior to the U.S. occupation that began at noon on August 12, 1898, is a Hawaiian subject. Hawaiian law recognizes all others who possess the nationality of their parents as part of the alien population. This greatly affects the political position of aboriginal Hawaiians today, who constituted nearly 85% of the Hawaiian citizenry in the 1890 census and who must still be considered so today despite being only approximately 20% of the current population in the Islands.

Despite the United States' violation of Hawai'i's sovereignty for over a century, international laws mandate that an occupying government administer the laws of the occupied State during the occupation, in a role similar to that of a trustee and beneficiary relationship.[6] Thus, the occupier cannot impose its own domestic laws without violating international law. This principle is clearly laid out in article 43 of the Hague Regulations, which states, "the authority of the legitimate power having in fact passed into the hands of the occupant, the latter shall take all the measures in his power to restore and ensure, as far as possible, public order and civil life, while respecting, unless absolutely prevented, the laws in force in the country." Referring to the American occupation of Hawai'i, Patrick Dumberry states:

> the 1907 Hague Convention protects the international personality of the occupied State, even in the absence of effectiveness. Furthermore, the legal order of the occupied State remains intact, although its effectiveness is greatly diminished by the fact of occupation. As such, Article 43 of the 1907 Hague Convention IV provides for the co-existence of two distinct legal orders, that of the occupier and the occupied.[7]

There are three distinct systems of law that exist in an occupied territory: "the indigenous law of the legitimate sovereign, to the extent that it has not been necessary to suspend it; the laws (legislation, orders, decrees, proclamations, and regulations) of the occupant, which are gradually introduced; and the applicable rules of customary and conventional international law."[8]

Hawai'i's sovereignty is maintained and protected by international law in spite of the absence of a diplomatically recognized government since 1893. In other words, the United States should have administered Hawaiian Kingdom law as defined by its constitution and statutory laws, similar to the U.S. military's administration of Iraqi law in Iraq with portions of the law suspended due to military necessity.[9] U.S. Army regulations on the law of occupation not only recognize the sovereignty of the occupied State, but also bar the annexation of the territory during hostilities because of the continuity of the invaded State's sovereignty. U.S. Army regulations on the laws of occupation not only recognize the continued existence of the sovereignty of the occupied State, but

confers upon the invading force the means of exercising control for the period of occupation. It does not transfer the sovereignty to the occupant, but simply the authority or power to exercise some of the rights of sovereignty. The exercise of these rights results from the established power of the occupant and from the necessity of maintaining law and order, indispensable both to the inhabitants and to the occupying force. It is therefore unlawful for a belligerent occupant to annex occupied territory or to create a new State therein while hostilities are still in progress.[10]

FM 27-10
DEPARTMENT OF THE ARMY FIELD MANUAL

THE LAW OF LAND WARFARE

DEPARTMENT OF THE ARMY · JULY 1956

U.S. Field Manual 27-10

International laws not only impose duties and obligations on an occupier, but also maintain and protect the international personality of the occupied State, notwithstanding the effectiveness and propaganda attributed to prolonged occupation.[11] Belligerent occupation "does not extinguish the State. And, generally, the *presumption*—in practice a strong one—is in favor of the continuance, and against the extinction, of an established State."[12] Therefore "the continuity of the Hawaiian Kingdom, in other words, may be refuted only by reference to a valid demonstration of legal title, or sovereignty, on the part of the United States.[13]

THE TERRITORY OF HAWAI'I

When the U.S. unilaterally annexed the Hawaiian Kingdom by a congressional joint resolution during the Spanish-American war, it violated not only the international laws of war, but also the 1893 *Lili'uokalani assignment* and *Agreement of Restoration*. On April 30, 1900, the U.S. Congress passed an Act establishing a civil government to be called the Territory of Hawai'i.[14] Regarding U.S. nationals, section 4 of the 1900 Act stated:

*U.S. Troops at Honolulu Harbor, 1898
(Hawai'i Archives)*

all persons who were citizens of the Republic of Hawai'i on August twelfth, eighteen hundred and ninety-eight, are hereby declared to be citizens of the United States and citizens of the Territory of Hawai'i. And all citizens of the United States resident in the Hawaiian Islands who were resident there on or since August twelfth, eighteen hundred and ninety-eight and all the citizens of the United States who shall hereafter reside in the Territory of Hawai'i for one year shall be citizens of the Territory of Hawai'i.[15]

Ocean Liner Arriving at Honolulu Harbor (Hawai'i Archives)

Under these U.S. laws, the putative population of U.S. "citizens" in the Hawaiian Kingdom exploded from a meager 1,928 (not including native Hawaiian nationals) out of a total population of 89,990 in 1890, to 423,174 (including native Hawaiians, who were now "citizens" of the U.S.) out of a total population of 499,794 in 1950.[16] The native Hawaiian population, which accounted for 85% of the total citizenry in 1890, accounted for a mere 20% (only 86,091 of 423,174) of the total population by 1950.[17]

According to international law, the migration of U.S. citizens to these islands, which included both military and civilian immigration, is a direct violation of Article 49 of the Fourth Geneva Convention, which provides that the occupying power shall not "transfer parts of its own civilian population into the territory it occupies."[18]

The purpose of Article 49 "is to protect the interests of the occupied population, rather than the population of the occupant."[19] Civilian migration and settlement in an occupied State are questionable under Article 43 of the Hague Regulation, since it cannot be "deemed a matter of security of the occupation forces, and it is even more difficult to demonstrate its contribution to 'public order and civil life.'"[20]

In 1946, the United States further misrepresented its relationship with Hawai'i in accordance with Article 73(e) of the United Nations Charter when the United States ambassador to the United Nations identified Hawai'i as a non-self-governing territory under the administration of the United States since 1898.[21]

Hawai'i should have never been placed on the list in the first place because it already achieved self-governance as a "sovereign independent State" in 1843—a recognition explicitly granted by the United States itself in 1844 and acknowledged by the 9th Circuit Court of Appeals in 2004.[22] It is clear that Hawai'i was deliberately treated as a non-self-governing territory or colonial possession in order to conceal the United States' prolonged occupation of an independent and sovereign State for military purposes.

The reporting of Hawai'i as a non-self-governing territory also coincided with the United States establishment of the headquarters for the Pacific Command (PACOM) on the Island of O'ahu. No doubt, if the United Nations had been aware of Hawai'i's continued legal status as an occupied neutral State, member States such as Russia and China would have prevented the United States from maintaining its military presence as a result of the Cold War.

The initial Article 73(e) list was comprised of non-sovereign territories under the control of sovereign States such as Australia, Belgium, Denmark, France, the Netherlands, New Zealand, the United Kingdom and the United States. In addition to Hawai'i, the U.S. also reported the territories of Alaska, American Samoa, Guam, the Panama Canal Zone, Puerto Rico and the Virgin Islands. The U.N. General Assembly resolution entitled "Principles which should guide Members in determining whether or not an obligation exists to transmit the information called for under Article 73(e) of the Charter," defined self-governance in three forms: a sovereign independent State; free association with an independent State; or integration with an independent State.[23] None of the territories on the list of non-self-governing territories, with the exception of Hawai'i, was recognized as a sovereign State.

THE STATE OF HAWAI'I

"For most people," wrote Tom Coffman, "the fiction of the Republic of Hawai'i successfully obscured the nature of the conquest, as it does to this day. The act of annexation became something that just happened."[24] The first statehood bill was introduced in Congress in 1919, but failed because Congress did not view the Hawaiian Islands as an incorporated territory. Island statehood advocates assumed the Hawaiian Islands were a part of the United States since 1898. However, it appears that they weren't aware of the Senate's secret session that clearly proved Hawai'i to be an occupied State, not an incorporated territory acquired by a treaty of cession.[25] Ironically, the legislature of the civil government in the Islands, without any knowledge of the Senate secret session transcripts, enacted a "Bill of Rights," on April 26, 1923, asserting their perceived right of becoming an American State of the Union.[26]

With the passage of this statute, residents in the Hawaiian Islands made a concerted effort to seek entry into the Federal union. The object of American statehood was finally accomplished when two special elections were held in the occupied kingdom. As a result of the elections, 63 delegates were elected to draft a constitution that was ratified on November 7, 1950.[27]

On March 12, 1959, the U.S. Congress approved the statehood bill and it was signed into law on March 15, 1959.[28] In a special election held on June 27, 1959, three propositions were submitted to vote. First, "shall Hawai'i immediately be admitted into the Union as a State?"; second, "the boundaries of the State of Hawai'i shall be as prescribed in the Act of Congress approved March 18, 1959, and all claims of this State to any areas of land or sea outside the boundaries prescribed are hereby irrevocably relin-

Hawai'i Statehood (Hawai'i Archives)

quished to the United States"; and third, "all provisions of the Act of Congress approved March 18, 1959, reserving rights or powers to the United States, as well as those prescribing the terms or conditions of the grants of lands or other property therein made to the State of Hawai'i are consented to fully by said State and its people."[29]

The residents of the Hawaiian Islands accepted all three propositions by 132,938 votes to 7,854. On July 28, 1959, two U.S. Hawai'i Senators and one Representative were elected to office, and on August 21, 1959, President Eisenhower proclaimed that the process of admitting Hawai'i as a State of the Federal union was complete, and the U.S. Ambassador reported to the United Nations that Hawai'i achieved self-governance as the 50th State of the Union.[30]

In 1988, acting U.S. Attorney General Douglas Kmiec raised questions in a legal opinion from the Office of Legal Counsel, U.S. Department of Justice, titled "Legal Issues Raised by Proposed Presidential Proclamation To Extend the Territorial Sea." While addressing constitutional matters on whether it is the President or the Congress that can extend the territorial seas of the United States from three to twelve miles, it also addressed the legality of congressional action in annexing the Hawaiian Islands by joint resolution, and also Congress' authority to establish boundaries for the State of Hawai'i that lie beyond the territorial seas of the United States' western coastline. Although Kmiec acknowledged Congressional authority to admit new States into the union and its inherent power to establish state boundaries, he did caution that it was the "President's constitutional status as the representative of the United States in foreign affairs," not Congress, "which authorizes the United States to claim territorial rights in the sea for the purpose of international law."[31]

CHAPTER 11
SOVERIGNTY MOVEMENT

*T*he *Hawaiian sovereignty* movement appears to have grown out of a social movement in the islands in the mid-20th century. According to one scholar, Lawrence Fuchs, "the essential purpose of the haole [foreigner] elite for four decades after annexation was to control Hawai'i; the major aim for the lesser haoles was to promote and maintain their privileged position…Most Hawaiians were motivated by a dominant and inclusive purpose—to recapture the past."[32]

Native Hawaiians were experiencing a sense of revival of Hawaiian culture, language, arts and music—euphoria of native Hawaiian pride. Momi Kamahele states, that "the ancient form of hula experienced a strong revival as the Native national dance for our own cultural purposes and enjoyment rather than as a service commodity for the tourist industry."[33] The sovereignty movement also resulted in the revitalization of "the Hawaiian language through immersion education."[34] John Dominis Holt, author of the 1964 book *On Being Hawaiian*, is credited for igniting the resurgence of native Hawaiian consciousness.[35]

> *I am a part-Hawaiian who has for years felt troubled concern over the loss of Hawaiian-ness or ethnic consciousness among people like ourselves. So much that came down to us was garbled or deliberately distorted. It was difficult to separate truth from untruth; to clarify even such simple matters for many among us as the maiden name of a Hawaiian grandmother, let alone know anything at all of the Hawaiian past.*[36]

Tom Coffman explained that when he "arrived in Hawai'i in 1965, the effective definition of history had been reduced to a few years. December 7, 1941, was practically the beginning of time, and anything that might have happened before that was prehistory."[37] Coffman admits that when he wrote his first book in 1970 he used Statehood in 1959 as an important benchmark in Hawaiian history.[38] The first sentence in chapter one of this book reads, the "year 1970 was only the eleventh year of statehood, so that as a state Hawai'i was still young, still enthralled by the right to self-government, still feeling out its role as America's newest state."[39] He recollected in a subsequent book:

> *Many years passed before I realized that for Native Hawaiians to survive as a people, they needed a definition of time that spanned something more than eleven years. The demand for a changed understanding of time was always implicit in what became known as the Hawaiian movement or the Hawaiian Renaissance because Hawaiians so systematically turned to the past whenever the subject of Hawaiian life was glimpsed.*[40]

The native Hawaiian community had been the subject of extreme prejudice and political exclusion since the United States imposed its authority in the Hawaiian Islands in 1898, and the history books that followed routinely portrayed the native Hawaiian as passive and inept. After the overthrow of the Hawaiian Kingdom the self-respect of native Hawaiians had been "undermined by carping criticism of 'Hawaiian beliefs' and stereotypes concerning our being lazy, laughing,

1898 Cartoon of School Begins—Puck Magazine (Hawai'i Archives)

lovable children who needed to be looked after by more 'realistic' adult-oriented caretakers came to be the new accepted view of Hawaiians."[41] This stereotyping became institutionalized, and is evidenced in the writings by Gavan Daws, an American historian, who wrote in 1974:

> *The Hawaiians had lost much of their reason for living long ago, when the kapus were abolished; since then a good many of them had lost their lives through disease; the survivors lost their land; they lost their leaders, because many of the chiefs withdrew from politics in favor of nostalgic self-indulgence; and now at last they lost their independence. Their resistance to all this was feeble. It was almost as if they believed what the white man said about them, that they had only half learned the lessons of civilization.*[42]

Although the Hawaiian Renaissance movement originally had no clear political objectives, it did foster a genuine sense of inquiry and thirst for an alternative Hawaiian history that was otherwise absent in contemporary history books. Political scientist, Noenoe Silva states, "When the stories can be validated, as happens when scholars read the literature in Hawaiian and make the findings available to the community, people begin to recover from the wounds caused by that disjuncture in their consciousness."[43]

As a result, Native Hawaiians began to draw meaning and political activism from a history that appeared to parallel other native peoples of the world who had been colonized, but the interpretive context of Hawaiian history was, at the time, primarily historical and not legal. State sovereignty and international laws were perceived not as a benefit for native peoples, but were seen as tools of the colonizer. According to James Anaya, who specializes in the rights of indigenous peoples, "international law was thus able to govern the patterns of colonization and ultimately to legitimate the colonial order."[44]

NATIVE HAWAIIANS ASSOCIATE WITH PLIGHT OF NATIVE AMERICANS

Following the course Congress set in the 1971 Alaska Native Claims Settlement Act,[45] under which "the United States returned 40 million acres of land to the Alaskan natives and paid $1 billion cash for land titles they did not return,"[46] it became common practice for Native Hawaiians to associate themselves with the plight of Native Americans and other ethnic minorities through-out the world who had been colonized and dominated by Europe or the United States.[47]

The Hawaiian Renaissance gradually branched out to include a political wing often referred to as the "sovereignty movement," which evolved into political resistance against U.S. sovereignty. As native Hawaiians began to organize, their political movement "paralleled the activism surround-ing the civil rights movement, women's liberation, student uprisings and the anti-Vietnam War movement."[48]

Protect Kahoʻolawe ʻOhana Poster
(Hawaiʻi Archives)

In 1972, an organization called A.L.O.H.A. (Aboriginal Lands of Hawaiian Ancestry) was founded to seek reparations from the United States for its involvement in the illegal overthrow of the Hawaiian Kingdom government in 1893.[49] Frustrated with inaction by the United States it joined another group called *Hui Ala Loa* (Long Road Organization) and formed *Protect Kahoʻolawe ʻOhana* (P.K.O.) in 1975.[50] P.K.O. was organized to stop the U.S. Navy from utilizing the island of Kahoʻolawe, off the southern coast of Maui, as a target range by openly occupying the island in defiance of the U.S. military. The U.S. Navy had been using the entire island as a target range for naval gunfire since World War II, and as a result of P.K.O.'s activism, the Navy terminated its use of the island in 1994.

Another organization called *'Ohana O Hawai'i* (Family of Hawai'i), formed in 1974, even went to the extreme measure of proclaiming a declaration of war against the United States of America.[51]

The political movements also served as the impetus for native Hawaiians to participate in the State of Hawai'i's Constitutional Convention in 1978, which resulted in the creation of the Office of Hawaiian Affairs (O.H.A.).[52] O.H.A. recognizes two definitions of aboriginal Hawaiian: the term "native Hawaiian" with a lower case "n," and "Native Hawaiian" with an upper case "N," both of which were established by the U.S. Congress.[53] The former is defined by the 1921 Hawaiian Homestead Commission Act as "any descendant of not less than one-half part of the blood of the races inhabiting the Hawaiian Islands previous to 1778," while the latter is defined by the 1993 Apology Resolution as "any individual who is a descendent of the aboriginal people who, prior to 1778, occupied and exercised sovereignty in the area that now constitutes the State of Hawai'i." The intent of the Apology resolution was to offer an apology to all Native Hawaiians, without regard to blood quantum, while the Hawaiian Homes Commission Act's definition was intended to limit those receiving homestead lots to be "not less than one-half" of native Hawaiian descent by blood. O.H.A. states that it serves both definitions of Hawaiian.[54] As a governmental agency, O.H.A.'s mission is to:

> ...malama (protect) Hawai'i's people and environmental resources and OHA's assets, toward ensuring the perpetuation of the culture, the enhancement of lifestyle and the protection of entitlements of Native Hawaiians, while enabling the building of a strong and healthy Hawaiian people and nation, recognized nationally and internationally.

Sovereignty Group (Honolulu Weekly)

The sovereignty movement created a multitude of diverse groups, each having an agenda as well as varying interpretations of Hawaiian history. Operating within an ethnic or tribal optic stemming from the Native-American movement in the United States, the sovereignty movement in Hawai'i eventually expanded itself to become a part of the global movement of indigenous peoples who reject colonial "arrangements in exchange for indigenous modes of self-determination that sharply curtail the legitimacy and jurisdiction of the State while bolstering indigenous jurisdiction over land, identity and political voice."[55]

Haunani-Kay Trask, an indigenous peoples' rights advocate, argues that "documents like the Draft Declaration [of Indigenous Human Rights] are used to transform and clarify public discussion and agitation." Specifically, Trask states that, "legal terms of reference, indigenous human rights concepts in international usage, and the political linkage of the non-self-governing status of the Hawaiian nation with other non-self-governing indigenous nations move Hawaiians into a world arena where Native peoples are primary and dominant states are secondary to the discussion."[56]

This political wing of the renaissance is not in any way connected to the legal position that the Hawaiian Kingdom continued to exist as a sovereign State under international law, but rather focuses on the history of European and American colonialism and the prospect of decolonization. As a result, sovereignty is not viewed as a legal reality, but a political aspiration.

The "Hawaiian sovereignty movement is now clearly the most potent catalyst for change," and "during the late 1980s and early 1990s sovereignty was transformed from an outlandish idea propagated by marginal groups into a legitimate political position supported by a majority of native Hawaiians."[57] The political activism relied on the normative framework of the developing rights of indigenous peoples within the United States and at the United Nations. At both these levels, indigenous peoples were viewed not as sovereign states, but rather "any stateless group" residing within the territorial dominions of existing sovereign states.[58]

Officials of the UCC, January 17, 1993 — Reverend Dr. Paul Sherry, President of the UCC (center) with wife, Mary (left) and Reverend James Kimo Merseberg (right) (photo Holly Henderson)

When the General Synod of the United Church of Christ (UCC) passed a resolution "Recognizing the Rights of Native Hawaiians to Self-Governance and Self-determination" in 1991, it was heralded as the beginning of a reconciliatory process between native and non-native Hawaiians for the 1893 overthrow of the Hawaiian Kingdom government. This resolution prompted the President of the UCC, in 1993, to issue a formal apology and committed the church to redress the wrongs done to native Hawaiians. Professor Andrew H. Walsh, who was commissioned by the UCC's Sovereignty Project to assist UCC officials in preparing a statement of apology in 1993, found that certain members of the Hawaiian Evangelical Association were complicit in the overthrow of the Hawaiian Kingdom government:

The Christian church founded by American missionaries in Hawai'i played no direct role in the Hawaiian Revolution of 1893. The Hawaiian Evangelical Association was, however, clearly under the control of white leaders who backed the revolution and attempted—at some cost—to influence indigenous Hawaiians to accept its outcome. The church's leaders endorsed the revolution in their correspondence with Congregational officials in the United States and vigorously attempted to enlist American Protestant support for annexation. In addition, several individual ministers of the HEA played active roles as advocates of the revolution to the American public.[59]

The UCC's *Redress Plan* included multi-million dollar reparations and the transference of six parcels of land on five islands to Native Hawaiian churches, the Association of Hawaiian Evangelical Churches, and the Pūʻā Foundation.[60] Eric Yamamoto, a legal expert in reconciliation, views these reconciliatory efforts by the UCC within the framework of post-colonial theory in post-civil rights America, and focuses on interracial justice for Native Hawaiians within the United States legal system—an approach similar to the "United States' 1988 apology to and monetary reparations for Japanese Americans wrongfully interned during World War II."[61] Yamamoto and other contemporary scholars, view the U.S. takeover of the Hawaiian Islands as *fait accompli*—a history and consequence no different than other colonial takeovers throughout the world of indigenous people and their lands by western powers.[62]

The UCC apology also prompted the Congress to pass a joint resolution in 1993 apologizing only to the Native Hawaiian people, rather than to the entire citizenry of the Hawaiian Kingdom, for the United States' role in the overthrow of the Hawaiian government.[63] This resolution maintained an indigenous and historically inaccurate focus that implied that only ethnic Hawaiians constituted the kingdom, and fertilized the incipient ethnocentrism of the sovereignty movement. The Resolution provided:

> Congress…apologizes to the Native Hawaiians on behalf of the people of the United States for the overthrow of the Kingdom of Hawai'i on January 17, 1893 with the participation of agents and citizens of the United States, and the deprivation of the rights of Native Hawaiians to self-determination.[64]

The Congressional apology rallied many Native Hawaiians, who were not fully aware of the legal status of the Hawaiian Islands as a sovereign State, in the belief that their situation had similar qualities to Native-American tribes in the nineteenth century. The resolution reinforced the belief of a native Hawaiian nation grounded in Hawaiian indigeneity and culture, rather than an occupied State under prolonged occupation.

Consistent with the Apology Resolution, Senator Akaka attempted five times since 2000 to have the Senate pass a bill that would provide for federal recognition of tribal status for Native Hawaiians. On February 4, 2009, he reintroduced Senate Bill 381 for the sixth time, known as the Akaka Bill, to the 111th Congress. According to Akaka, the bill's purpose is to provide "a process within the framework of Federal law for the Native Hawaiian people to exercise their inherent rights as a distinct aboriginal, indigenous, native community to reorganize a Native Hawaiian government for the purpose of giving expression to their rights as native people to self-determination and self-governance."[65]

According to Rupert Emerson, an international law scholar, there are two major periods when the international community accepted self-determination as an operative right or principle.[66] President Woodrow Wilson and others first applied the principle to nations directly affected by the "defeat or collapse of the German, Russian, Austro-Hungarian and Turkish land empires" after the First World War.[67] The second period took place after the Second World War and the United Nations' focus on disintegrating overseas empires of its member states, "which had remained effectively untouched in the round of Wilsonian self-determination."[68]

These territories have come to be known as Mandate, Trust, and Article 73(e) territories under the United Nations Charter. Because Native Hawaiians were erroneously categorized as a stateless people, the principle of self-determination would underlie the development of legislation such as the Akaka bill.

The Akaka bill's identification of Native Hawaiians as an indigenous people with a right to self-determination relies upon the U.S. National Security Council's position on indigenous peoples. On January 18, 2001, the Council made known its position to its delegations assigned to the "U.N. Commission on Human Rights," the "Commission's Working Group on the United Nations (UN) Draft Declaration on Indigenous Rights," and to the "Organization of American States (OAS) Working Group to Prepare the Proposed American Declaration on the Rights of Indigenous Populations." The Council directed these delegates to "read a prepared statement that expresses the U.S. understanding of the term internal 'self-determination' and indicates that it does not include a right of independence or permanent sovereignty over natural resources."[69]

The Council also directed these delegates to support the use of the term *internal self-determination* in both the U.N. and O.A.S. declarations on indigenous rights, and defined Indigenous Peoples as having "a right of internal self-determination." By virtue of that right, "they may negotiate their political status within the framework of the existing nation-state and are free to pursue their economic, social, and cultural development.[70] This resolution sought to constrain the growing political movement of indigenous peoples "who aspire to rule their territorial homeland, or who claim the right to independent statehood under the doctrine of self-determination of peoples."[71] The Akaka bill falsely identifies native Hawaiians and their right to self-determination under the U.S. National Security Council's definition.

DISTINCTION BETWEEN OCCUPATION AND INDIGENEITY

International law provides an appropriate lens to the political and legal history of the Hawaiian Islands, which has been relegated under U.S. sovereignty and the right to internal self-determination of indigenous peoples. There are inherent contradictions and divergence of thought and direction between the concepts of Hawaiian State sovereignty and Hawaiian indigeneity.

Hawaiian State Sovereignty	vs.	Hawaiian Indigeneity
Self-governing		Non-self-governing
Independent		Dependent
Sovereignty Established		Sovereignty Sought
Citizenship (multi-ethnic)		Indigenous (mono-ethnic)
Occupation		Colonization
De-Occupation		De-Colonization

The legal definition of a *colony* is "a dependent political economy, consisting of a number of citizens of the same country who have emigrated therefrom to people another, and remain subject to the mother country."[72] According to Albert Keller, a colonial studies scholar, *colonization* is "a movement of population and an extension of political power," and therefore must be distinguished from migration.[73]

Colonization is an extension of sovereignty over territory not subject to the sovereignty of another State, while migration is the mode of entry into the territory of another sovereign State. The "so-called 'interior colonization' of the Germans [within a non-German State] would naturally be a misnomer on the basis of the definition suggested."[74] This would suggest that the migration of United States citizens into the territory of the Hawaiian Kingdom constituted American colonization and somehow resulted in the creation of an American colony.

The history of the Hawaiian Kingdom has fallen victim to the misuse of this term by contemporary scholars in the fields of post-colonial and cultural studies. These scholars have lost sight of the original use and application of the terms colony and colonization, and have remained steadfast in their conclusion that the American presence in the Hawaiian Islands was and is currently colonial in nature. This erroneous use of the word has caused much confusion and complicates agreement on legal and political solutions.

Slavoj Zizek, a philosophy scholar, critically suggests that in post-colonial studies, the use of the term colonization "starts to function as a hegemonic notion and is elevated to a universal paradigm, so that in relations between the sexes, the male sex colonizes the female sex, the upper classes colonize the lower classes, and so on."[75] He argues that in cultural studies it "effectively functions as a kind of *ersatz*-philosophy, and notions are thus transformed into ideological universals."[76]

In the legal and political realm, the fundamental difference between the terms *colonization/ de-colonization* and *occupation/de-occupation*, is that the colonized must negotiate with the colonizer in order to acquire state sovereignty, e.g. India from Great Britain, Rwanda from Belgium, and Indonesia from the Dutch. Under the latter, State sovereignty is presumed and not dependent on the will of the occupier, e.g. Soviet occupation of the Baltic States, and the American occupation of Afghanistan and Iraq. *Colonization/de-colonization* is a matter that concerns the internal laws of the colonizing State and presumes the colony is not sovereign, while *occupation/de-occupation* is a matter of international law relating to already existing sovereign States. Matthew Craven an international law scholar who has done extensive research on the continuity of the Hawaiian State, concludes:

> *For the Hawaiian sovereignty movement, therefore, acceding to their identification as an indigenous people would be to implicitly accede not only to the reality, but also to the legitimacy, of occupation and political marginalization. All they might hope for at that level is formal recognition of their vulnerability and continued political marginalization rather than the status accorded under international law to a nation belligerently occupied.*[77]

Hawaiian State sovereignty and the international laws of occupation not only presume the continuity of Hawaiian sovereignty, but also provide the legal framework for regulating the occupier, despite its history of non-compliance. It is clear that the U.S. government wrongfully administered the Hawaiian Islands since 1898 as if it were a colonial possession for the purpose of concealing a gross violation of international law. Therefore, colonialism must be viewed as a tool used by the occupant to commit fraud in an attempt to extinguish the memory of sovereignty and the legal order of the occupied State.

Self-determination, inherent sovereignty and indigenous peoples are terms fundamentally linked not just to the concept, but to the political and legal process of de-colonization, which presupposes sovereignty to be an aspiration and not a legal reality. The effects of colonization have affected the psychological and physiological make-up of many native Hawaiians, but these effects must be reinterpreted through the lens of international law. Colonial treatment is the evidence of the violation of the law, not the political basis of a sovereignty movement. As such, these violations should serve as the measurement for reparations and compensation to a people who, against all odds, fought and continue to fight to maintain their dignity, health, language and culture, and above all, their rightful and lawful sovereign status.

In 2009, a revised edition of *Nation Within* by Coffman was published with a significant change in its subtitle.[78] In the original version published in 1998, the subtitle reads "The Story of America's Annexation of the Nation of Hawai'i," but the revised edition now reads "The History of the American Occupation of Hawai'i." Coffman explains:

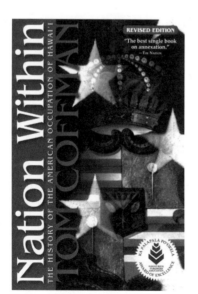

Nation Within, by Tom Coffman, revised edition 2009

In the book's subtitle, the word Annexation *has been replaced by the word* Occupation, *referring to America's occupation of Hawai'i. Where annexation connotes legality by mutual agreement, the act was not mutual and therefore not legal. Since by definition of international law there was no annexation, we are left then with the word occupation. In making this change, I have embraced the logical conclusion of my research into the events of 1893 to 1898 in Honolulu and Washington, D.C. I am prompted to take this step by a growing body of historical work by a new generation of Native Hawaiian scholars.[79]*

CHAPTER 12
THE LAW OF OCCUPATION

Occupation does not change the legal order of the occupied State, and according to Krystyna Marek, an international law scholar, there is "nothing the occupant can legally do to break the continuity of the occupied State. He cannot annul its laws; he can only prevent their implementation. He cannot destitute judges and officials; he can merely prevent them from exercising their functions."[80] These constraints upon the occupier, as formulated in Article 43 of the Hague Regulations, compel the occupying State "to respect the existing—and continuing—legal order of the occupied State."[81] Chapter II, section 6 of the Hawaiian Civil Code, provides:

> *The laws are obligatory upon all persons, whether subjects of this kingdom, or citizens or subjects of any foreign State, while within the limits of this kingdom, except so far as exception is made by the laws of nations in respect to Ambassadors or others. The property of all such persons, while such property is within the territorial jurisdiction of this kingdom, is also subject to the laws.*[82]

The term obligatory does not import a choice, but rather a mandate or legal constraint to bind.[83] According to Sir William R. Anson, a legal scholar, "obligation is a power of control, exercisable by one person over another, with reference to future and specified acts or forbearances."[84] It is a fundamental aspect of compliance that lays down the duty of all persons "while within the limits of this kingdom," and forms the basis of the legal order of the Hawaiian Kingdom—allegiance. According to John Bouvier, an American jurist, allegiance is the tie, "which binds the citizen to the government, in return for the protection which the government affords."[85] It is also the duty, "which the subject owes to the sovereign, correlative with the protection received."[86] A duty not just owed by the subjects of the state, but also by all persons within its territory to include aliens. Hawaiian penal law, in particular, defines allegiance to be "the obedience and fidelity due to the kingdom from those under its protection."[87] The statute also provides that an "alien, whether his native country be at war or at peace with this kingdom, owes allegiance to this kingdom during his residence therein."[88]

THE CIVIL POPULATION OF AN OCCUPIED STATE

As allegiance is the essential tie between the government and the governed, without which there is anarchy, a question will naturally arise on whether or not the duty of a population's allegiance is affected in any way when its government has been overthrown and replaced by a foreign occupational government. European practice in the seventeenth and eighteenth century treated occupied territories as annexed territories, and, therefore, the inhabitants were forced to swear an oath of allegiance, but this practice changed as a result of the evolution of international law and the maintenance of the legal order of an occupied State.

By the early nineteenth century, "Anglo-American courts defined the relationship of native inhabitants to the occupant as one of temporary allegiance."[89] According to international law scholar Henry Halleck, "the duty of allegiance is reciprocal to the duty of protection," and, therefore, when "a state is unable to protect…its territory from the superior force of an enemy, it loses, for the time, its claim to the allegiance of those whom it fails to protect, and the inhabitants of the conquered territory pass under a temporary or qualified allegiance to the conqueror."[90] In recent times, however, Gerhard von Glahn, a political scientist, states, "there seems to have been a change in point of view, and it can be said that, at the most, the inhabitants should give an obedience equal to that previously given to the laws of their legitimate sovereign and that, at the least, they should obey the occupant to the extent that such result can be enforced through the latter's military supremacy."[91]

The next logical question would be whether or not the laws of occupation affect or modify the domestic laws of the occupied state, which the Hawaiian Civil Code holds as obligatory. Article 43 of the Hague Regulations provides that the laws of the occupied State must be administered. According to former U.S. Assistant Secretary of State David J. Hill, "the intention of the regulations is that the order and economy of civil life be disturbed as little as possible by the fact of military occupation; which is not directed against individuals or against society as an institution, but solely against armed resistance."[92] This requirement for the occupant to respect the laws of the occupied State, also means that the occupant does not have to respect the laws if there are extenuating circumstances that absolutely prevents it, e.g. military necessity.

International law scholar, Eyal Benvenisti, states that, "the drafters of [Article 43] viewed military necessity as the sole relevant consideration that could 'absolutely prevent' an occupant from maintaining the old order."[93] Therefore, there must be a balance between the security interest of the occupant against hostilities by the forces of the occupied State, which they are at war with, and the protection of the interests of the occupied population by maintaining "public order and safety." This was precisely stated in 1907 by a United States Court of Claims in *Ho Tung and Co. v. The United States* regarding the collection of duties by U.S. military authorities at the port of Manila during the Spanish-American War. The court held that "It is unquestioned that upon the occupation by our military forces of the port of Manila it was their duty to respect and assist in enforcing the municipal laws then in force there until the same might be changed by order of the military commander, called for by the necessities of war."[94] However, von Glahn expands the occupant's lawmaking capacity beyond war measures, and includes laws necessitated by the interests of the local population:

> …*the secondary aim of any lawful military occupation is the safeguarding of the welfare of the native population, and this secondary and lawful aim would seem to supply the necessary basis for such new laws as are passed by the occupant for the benefit of the*

population and are not dictated by his own military necessity and requirements.[95]

American practice has divided military jurisdiction into three parts—military law, military government and martial law. Military law is exercised over military personnel, whether or not the military bases are situated within U.S. territory or abroad; military government is exercised over occupied territories of a foreign State; and martial law is exercised over U.S. citizens and residents within U.S. territory during emergencies. Military government, therefore, is a matter of international law and the rules of war on land, while martial law is a matter of U.S. municipal law.[96] According to U.S. constitutional law, martial law is declared when U.S. civil law has been suspended by necessity and replaced by the orders of a military commander. These orders, whether they are lawful or not, are judged after the civil authority has been reinstated. Legislation emanating from a military government in occupied States, however, is not judged by the restored civil authority of an occupied State, but by the international laws of occupation. This subject is fully treated by Benvenisti, who states:

> *The occupant may not surpass its limits under international law through extraterritorial prescriptions emanating from its national institutions: the legislature, government, and courts. The reason for this rule is, of course, the functional symmetry, with respect to the occupied territory, among the various lawmaking authorities of the occupying state. Without this symmetry, Article 43 could become almost meaningless as a constraint upon the occupant, since the occupation administration would then choose to operate through extraterritorial prescription of its national institutions.*[97]

According to the U.S. Army and Navy Manual of Military Government and Civil Affairs during the Second World War, "military government must be established either by reason of military necessity as a right under international law, or as an obligation under international law."[98] Orders and legislation from a military government can only be sustained as long as the military government remains in effective control of the occupied territory. However, these laws lose all effect once the occupation comes to a close, and it is the sole decision of the restored government on whether or not to maintain those laws. Unlike U.S. constitutional law which recognizes governmental acts of a failed rebellion as long as it "had no connection with the disloyal resistance to government,"[99] international law does not mandate a restored government to respect the legislation made by a military government because a returning sovereign has far-reaching rescinding powers.[100]

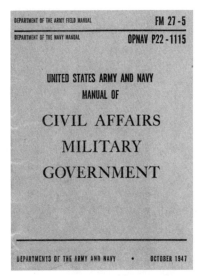

U.S. Army & Navy Field Manual 27-5

Three important facts resonate in the American occupation of the Hawaiian Kingdom. First, the Hawaiian Kingdom was never at war with the United States and as a subject of international law was a neutral state; second, there was never a military government established by the United States to administer Hawaiian law; and, third, all laws enacted by the Federal government and the State of Hawai'i, to include its predecessor the Territory of Hawai'i since 1900, stem from the law-making power of the United State Congress, which, by operation of United States constitutional constraints as well as Article 43, have no extraterritorial force. In other words, there has been no legitimate government, whether *de jure* or *de facto* under Hawaiian law or military law by the executive authority of the U.S. President, operating within the occupied State of the Hawaiian Kingdom since the illegal overthrow of the Hawaiian government on January 17th 1893; nor has there been any Hawaiian government in exile. All laws emanating from the national institutions of the United States have no legal effect within the occupied territory, and while governments are matters of a state's domestic law, "international law nevertheless has some bearing on it where a government is created in breach of international law, or is the result of an international illegality."[101]

In the 1930s, the international doctrine of non-recognition arose out of the principle that legal rights cannot derive from an illegal situation (*ex injuria jus non oritur*), which Professor Lassa Oppenheim calls "an inescapable principle of law."[102] In particular, the doctrine came about as a result of the Japanese invasion of Manchuria in 1931 and the setting up of a puppet government. After the invasion, U.S. Secretary of State Henry Stimson declared that "the illegal invasion would not be recognized as it was contrary to the 1928 Pact of Paris (the Kellog-Briand Pact) which had outlawed war as an instrument of national policy."[103] The non-recognition doctrine came to be known as the Stimson doctrine, and according to Professor Malcolm Shaw:

> *The role of non-recognition as an instrument of sanction as well as a means of pressure and a method of protecting the wronged inhabitants of a territory was discussed more fully in the Advisory Opinion of the International Court of Justice in the Namibia case, 1971, dealing with South Africa's presence in that territory. The Court held that since the continued South African occupancy was illegal, member states of the United Nations were obliged to recognize that illegality and the invalidity of South Africa's acts concerning Namibia and were under a duty to refrain from any actions implying recognition of the legality of, or lending support or assistance to, the South African presence and administration.*[104]

Marek explains that puppet governments "commit, for the benefit of the occupying power, all unlawful acts which the latter does not want to commit openly and directly. Such acts may range from mere violations of the occupation regime in the occupied, but still surviving State to a disguised annexation."[105] In 1938, Maximilian Litvinov, Russian Commissar for Foreign Affairs, reminded the League of Nations that there are cases of annexations "camouflaged by the setting-up of puppet 'national' governments, allegedly independent, but in reality serving merely as a screen for, and an agency of, the foreign invader."[106] The very aim of establishing puppet governments is "to enable the occupant to act in *fraudem legis*, to commit violations of the international regime of occupation in a disguised and indirect form, in other words, to disregard the firmly established principle of the identity and continuity of the occupied State."[107]

The most prominent feature of puppet governments "is that they are in no way related to the legal order of the occupied State; in other words, they are neither its government, nor its organ of any sort, and they do not carry on its continuity."[108] The U.S. Department of the Army affirms this understanding of puppet regimes. In its field manual on the Law of Land Warfare, it provides that the "restrictions placed upon the authority of a [military] government cannot be avoided by a system of using a puppet government, central or local, to carry out acts which would be unlawful if performed directly by the occupant. Acts induced or compelled by the occupant are nonetheless its acts."[109] The U.S. military never established a military government, but rather utilized puppet governments since 1893 to do their biddings in violation of international law.

The provisional government, Republic of Hawai'i, U.S. Territory of Hawai'i and the U.S. State of Hawai'i were all governments created out of an "international illegality." In the investigation of the 1893 overthrow, President Cleveland concluded the provisional government was "neither *de facto* nor *de jure*,"[110] but self-declared, and the U.S. Congress also concluded that the provisional government's successor, the Republic of Hawai'i, was also "self-declared."[111]

The question, however, is what was the status of the Territorial government (1900-1959) and the State of Hawai'i government (1959-present), both of which were not self-declared, but established by Congressional statute? Clearly the creation of these political institutions circumvented the duty of administering Hawaiian Kingdom laws during the occupation, and as such they can be argued to be puppet regimes illegally imposed in the occupied territory of the Hawaiian Kingdom, especially in light of the territorial limit of congressional authority. "Therefore, in response to contemporary challenges regarding the failure to fulfill the duty to establish a direct system of administration in an occupied territory:

> *...any measures whatsoever introduced by the occupant or its illegal surrogates would merit no respect in international law. The illegality of the occupation regime would taint all its measures, and render them null and void. The occupant who fails to establish the required regime does not seek international protection for its policies in the occupied area, and, indeed, is not entitled to expect any deference for these policies.*[112]

THE CASE FOR REPARATIONS

In 1983, the subject of reparations was taken up by the Native Hawaiian Studies Commission, established by an Act of Congress in 1980,[113] which "found no present legal entitlement to compensation for any loss of sovereignty."[114] This conclusion was due to the Commission's erroneous comparison of Hawai'i's sovereignty to how "United States courts have examined the concept of sovereignty for Indian tribes and that consideration would be applicable as well to native Hawaiians."[115] International laws, as they were applied to sovereign and independent States in the nineteenth century, were not applied because the Commission limited its investigation regarding sovereignty to when the Congress began to assert authority over the islands in 1898, by virtue of a joint resolution of annexation. The commission concluded:

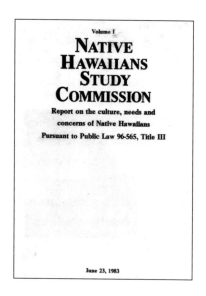

> For native groups, including Indian tribes and native Hawaiians, sovereignty 'exists only at the sufferance of Congress and is subject to complete defeasance.' In short, Congress can take away sovereignty of native groups at will, once it exercises sovereignty over the group. In terms of native Hawaiians, the United States was dealing with the government of Hawai'i as another sovereign until 1898. Courts will not look behind the United States' recognition of a foreign government; so before 1898, no action of Congress could be regarded as taking the sovereignty of Hawai'i.[116]

In 1993, the United Church of Christ and the Congress apologized for their participation in the overthrow of the Hawaiian Kingdom government and called for reconciliation, without restitution, between Native Hawaiians and the Church, Congress and the President of the United States. With the recently growing academic work at the University of Hawai'i at Manoa regarding the legal status of the Hawaiian Kingdom under international law, it has resulted in challenging long standing assumptions of the legal and political history of the Hawaiian Islands. These findings have called into question not just the basis of these reconciliatory initiatives, but the prospect of *reconciliation* itself as it relates to the current generation of Hawaiians, who, since 1843 and by definition under international law, remain nationals of an already existing State since 1843 that is "belligerently occupied,"[117] and continues to be illegally occupied and thus clearly are not members of a non-self-governing nation situated *within* the United States.

According to George Davis, an international law scholar, a *State* is "a society of persons having a permanent political organization, and exercising within a certain territory the usual functions of government,"[118] whereas a *Nation* "involves the idea of a community of race or language."[119] Only the latter has a right of self-determination, whom U. Oji Umozurike, a Nigerian international law scholar, defines as a right of a people "to determine their political future and freely pursue their economic, social, and cultural development [which] is manifested through independence, as well as self-government, local autonomy, merger, association, or some other participation in government."[120] In other words, since Native Hawaiians had already exercised their right of self-determination in 1843 and established a sovereign State for themselves, they are no longer non-self-governing but a self-governing country with a right to maintain their independence as a subject of international law. A people do not exercise their right to self-determination twice in order to achieve what was already achieved—independence.[121]

According to international law, restitution in kind, compensation and satisfaction, are forms of reparations afforded to an injured party, and can be imposed either singularly or collectively depending on the circumstances of the case. There are two recognized systems that provide reparations to an injured party—*remedial justice* where the injured party is a State, and *restorative justice* where the injured party or parties are individuals within a State. Remedial justice addresses compensation and punitive actions, while restorative justice uses reconciliation that attends "to the negative consequences of one's action through apology, reparation and penance."

International law is founded on remedial justice, whereas individual States, sometimes with the assistance of the United Nations, employ or facilitate varying forms of restorative justice within their territorial borders where "previously divided groups will come to agree on a mutually satisfactory narrative of what they have been through, opening the way to a common future."[122] The Guatemalan Historical Clarification Commission is an example of a restorative justice system, which was "established in 1996 as part of the UN-supervised peace accord." The Commission's function was to describe "the nature and scope of human rights abuses during the 30-year civil war."[123] An example of remedial justice is the 1927 seminal *Chorzow Factory* case (Germany v. Poland) heard before the Permanent Court of International Justice in The Hague, Netherlands, and described by Professor Dinah Shelton as "the cornerstone of international claims for reparation, whether presented by states or other litigants."[124] In that case, the court set forth the basic principles governing reparations after breaching an international obligation. The court stated:

Permanent Court of Internation Justice

> *The essential principle contained in the actual notion of an illegal act —a principle which seems to be established by international practice and in particular by the decisions of arbitral tribunals—is that reparation must, so far as possible, wipe-out all the consequences of the illegal act and reestablish the situation which would, in all probability, have existed if that act had not been committed. Restitution in kind, or, if this is not possible, payment of a sum corresponding to the value which a restitution in kind would bear; the award, if need be, of damages for loss sustained which would be covered by restitution in kind*

or payment in place of it—such are the principles which should serve to determine the amount of compensation due for an act contrary to international law.[125]

For the past century, scholars have viewed the overthrow of the Hawaiian government as irreversible and the annexing of the Hawaiian Islands as an extension of U.S. territory legally brought about by a congressional resolution. As a benign verb, the term annexation conjures up synonyms such as affix, append, incorporate or bring together. But recent study of this annexation reveals that it was not benign. Hawai'i's territory was occupied for military purposes and in the absence of any evidence extinguishing Hawaiian sovereignty, e.g. a treaty of cession, international laws not only impose duties and obligations on an occupier, but maintains and protects the international personality of the occupied State, despite the overthrow of its government. As an operative agency of the United States, its government "is that part of a state which undertakes the actions that, attributable to the state, are subject to regulation by the application of the principles and rules of international law."[126]

Ian Brownlie, a renowned scholar of international law, asserts that if "international law exists, then the dynamics of state sovereignty can be expressed in terms of law, and, as states are equal and have legal personality, sovereignty is in a major aspect a relation to other states (and to organizations of states) defined by law."[127] Restitutio in integrum is the basic principle and primary right of redress for states whose rights have been violated,[128] for "it is a principle of international law and even a general conception of law, that any breach of an engagement involves an obligation to make reparation."[129] Gerald Fitzmaurice, an international law scholar, argues that the "notion of international responsibility would be devoid of content if it did not involve a liability to 'make reparation in an adequate form.'"[130]

When an international law has been violated, the American Law Institute's *Restatement of the Foreign Relations Law of the United States* emphasizes the "forms of redress that will undo the effect of the violation, such as restoration of the status quo ante, restitution, or specific performance of an undertaking."[131] "In the case...of unlawful annexation of a State," according to James Crawford, an international law scholar, "the withdrawal of the occupying State's forces and the annulment of any decree of annexation may be seen as involving cessation rather than restitution. Even so, ancillary measures (the return of persons and property seized in the course of the invasion) will be required as an aspect either of cessation or restitution."[132] The underlying function of reparations, through remedial justice, is to restore the injured State to that position as if the injury had not taken place.

In 1948, the United Nations established the International Law Commission (ILC), comprised of legal experts from around the world that would fulfill the Charter's mandate of "encouraging the progressive development of international law and its codification."[133] State responsibility was one of fourteen topics selected for codification, and the ILC began its work in 1956. Codification, according to Brownlie, "involves the setting down, in a comprehensive and ordered form, of rules or existing law and the approval of the resulting text by a law-determining agency."[134]

U.N. Resolution on Responsibility of States for Internationally Wrongful Acts

On August 9, 2001, after nearly half a century, the ILC finally completed the articles on *Responsibility of States for Internationally Wrongful Acts*, and was faced with two options for action by the United Nations. According to Crawford, the ILC's *Special Rapporteur* for the articles and member of the commission since 1992, the articles could be the subject of "a convention on State responsibility and some form of endorsement or taking note of the articles by the General Assembly."[135]

Members of the Commission were divided on the options and decided upon a two-stage approach that would first get the General Assembly to take note of the articles, which were annexed to a resolution. After some reflection, the commission also recommended that a later session of the General Assembly would be best to consider the appropriateness and feasibility of a convention.[136] Crawford suggested that by having the General Assembly initially take note of the Articles by resolution, it could "commend it to States and to international courts and tribunals, leaving its content to be taken up in the normal processes of the application and development of international law."[137]

According to David Caron, a legal scholar of international law, the significance of the "work of the ILC is similar in authority to the writings of highly qualified publicists," and is a recognized source of international law.[138] In his fourth report on State Responsibility, Crawford stated, that "States, tribunals and scholars will refer to the text, whatever its status, because it will be an authoritative text in the field it covers."[139] There are two conceptual premises that underlie the articles of State responsibility:

1. The importance of upholding the rule of law in the interest of the international community as a whole; and
2. Remedial justice as the goal of reparations for those injured by the breach of an obligation.[140]

The codification of international law on State responsibility has been hailed as a major achievement "in the consolidation of the rule of law in international affairs." This is especially true because it "ventured out into the 'hard' field of law enforcement and sanctions, which has been classically considered the Achillean heel of international law."[141] Shelton also lauds, in particular, Article 41's mandate that States not only cooperate in order to bring to an end a serious breach of international law, but that States shall not "recognize as lawful a situation created by a serious breach."[142] Despite her view that the articles represent "the most far-reaching examples of the progressive development of international law,"[143] she admits it also highlights "the need to identify the means to satisfy injured parties while ensuring the international community's interest in promoting compliance."[144]

In 1991, though, the United Nations Security Council specifically addressed and established a means to satisfy injured parties who suffered from an international wrongful act by a State. After the first Gulf war, the Security Council established the *United Nations Compensation Commission* as "a new and innovative mechanism to collect, assess and ultimately provide compensation for hundreds of thousands—or even millions—of claims against Iraq for direct losses stemming from the invasion and occupation of Kuwait."[145] According to United Nations' Secretary General Kofi Annan, "the Commission is not a court or an arbitral tribunal before which the parties appear; it is a political organ that performs an essentially fact-finding function of examining claims, verifying their validity, evaluating losses, assessing payments and resolving disputed claims; it is only in this last respect that a quasi-judicial function may be involved."[146] Iraq's invasion and occupation of Kuwait was a violation of Kuwait's territorial integrity and sovereignty, and therefore considered an international wrongful act. It wasn't a dispute, so intervention of an international court or arbitral tribunal was not necessary.

An internationally wrongful act must be distinguished from a dispute between States. According to the *Responsibility of States for Internationally Wrongful Acts*, an international wrongful act consists of "an action or omission...attributable to the State under international law; and...constitutes a breach of an international obligation of the State."[147] A dispute, on the other hand, is "a disagreement on a point of law or fact, a conflict of legal views or of interests"[148] between two States. Conciliation, arbitration and judicial settlement settle legal disputes that seek to assert existing law, while negotiation, enquiry and mediation provide for the settlement of political disputes that deal with competing political or economic interests.[149] A claim by a State[150] becomes a dispute, whether legal or political, once the respondent State opposes the claim; but an internationally wrongful act is not dependent on a State's opposing claim, especially if the breach involves the violation of a peremptory norm or *jus cogens*.[151] International law scholar James Crawford explains:

> *Circumstances precluding wrongfulness are to be distinguished from other arguments which may have the effect of allowing a State to avoid responsibility. They have nothing to do with questions of the jurisdiction of a court or tribunal over a dispute or the admissibility of a claim. They are to be distinguished from the constituent requirements of the obligation, i.e. those elements which have to exist for the issue of wrongfulness to arise in the first place and which are in principle specified by the obligation itself.*[152]

In similar fashion, Hawai'i would find satisfaction through a compensation commission established by the United Nations Security Council that would be capable of addressing the subject of reparations and the effects of a prolonged and continuing occupation. As evidenced in its history, the Hawaiian Kingdom does not have a dispute with the United States that would require settlement by an international court or arbitral tribunal. Instead, we have over a century of violating the terms of the 1893 *Lili'uokalani assignment* and the *Agreement of restoration*, being sole executive agreements, and the international laws of occupation. Therefore, as an international wrongful act, the appropriate venue for remedy could be a matter of enforcement through the U.N. Security Council.

KEY CONCEPTS

State Sovereignty	Occupation/De-occupation	Nationality
Aliens	Non-self Governing	Self-determination
Indigenous People	Colonization/De-colonization	Sovereignty movement

FURTHER CONSIDERATION

1. According to international law, what are the duties of an occupying State in relation to the State that is being occupied?

2. Break up into groups and discuss amongst yourselves the establishment of the Territorial and State governments within the framework of international law? What is the source of these enactments and are there limits to Congressional authority in an occupied State?

3. What were the circumstances that created the sovereignty movement and is this movement a continuation of the political activism of Hawaiian subjects since the illegal overthrow of the Hawaiian Kingdom government or is it a new movement? Define indigeneity.

[1] William Addleman, *History of the United States Army in Hawai'i*, 1849-1939, (Hawai'i War Records Depository, Hamilton Library, University of Hawai'i, Manoa), 9.

[2] Ian Lind, "Ring of Steel: Notes on the Militarization of Hawai'i," *Social Process in Hawai'i* 31 (1984-85): 25-47, 25.

[3] U.S. Pacific Command was established in the Hawaiian Islands as a unified command on 1 January 1947, as an outgrowth of the command structure used during World War II. Located at Camp Smith, which overlooks Pearl Harbor on the island of O'ahu, the Pacific Command is headed by a four star Admiral who reports directly to the Secretary of Defense concerning operations and the Joint Chiefs of Staff for administrative purposes. That Admiral is the Commander-in-Chief, Pacific Command. The Pacific Command's responsibility stretches from North America's west coast to Africa's east coast and both the North and South Poles. It is the oldest and largest of the United States' nine unified military commands, and is comprised of Army, Navy, Marine Corps, and Air Force service components, all headquartered in Hawai'i. Additional commands that report to the Pacific Command include U.S. Forces Japan, U.S. Forces Korea, Special Operations Command Pacific, U.S. Alaska Command, Joint Task Force Full-Accounting, Joint Interagency Task Force West, the Asia-Pacific Center for Security Studies, and the Joint Intelligence Center Pacific in Pearl Harbor.

[4] Statute Laws of His Majesty Kamehameha III, vol. 1 (Government Press 1846), 76.

[5] Gehard von Glahn, *The Occupation of Enemy Territory: A Commentary on the Law and Practice of Belligerent Occupation* (University of Minnesota Press 1957), 60.

[6] Eyal Benvenisti, *The International Law of Occupation* (Princeton University Press 1993), 6; Gehard von Glahn, *Law Among Nations*, 6th ed. (Maxwell Macmillan Canada, Inc. 1992), 785-794; and von Glahn, Occupation of Enemy Territory, 95-221.

[7] Patrick Dumberry, "The Hawaiian Kingdom Arbitration Case and the Unsettled Question of the Hawaiian Kingdom's Claim to Continue as an Independent State under International Law," *Chinese Journal of International Law* 1(1)(2002): 655-684, 682.

[8] Von Glahn, *Law Among Nations*, 774.

[9] David J. Scheffer, "Beyond Occupation Law," *American Journal of International Law* 97(4) (October 2003): 842-860.

[10] "The Law of Land Warfare", *U.S. Army Field Manual* 27-10, (July 1956), §358.

[11] Regarding the principle of effectiveness in international law, Marek explains, "A comparison of the scope of the two legal orders, of the occupied and the occupying State, co-existing in one and the same territory and limiting each other, throws an interesting light on one aspect of the principle of effectiveness in international law. In the first place: of these two legal orders, that of the occupied State is regular and 'normal', while that of the occupying power is exceptional and limited. At the same time, the legal order of the occupant is, as has been strictly subject to the principle of effectiveness, while the legal order of the occupied State continues to exist notwithstanding the absence of effectiveness. It can produce legal effects outside the occupied territory and may even develop and expand, not by reason of its effectiveness, but solely on the basis of the positive international rule safeguarding its continuity. Thus, the relation between effectiveness and title seems to be one of inverse proportion: while a strong title can survive a period of non-effectiveness, a weak title must rely heavily, if not exclusively, on full and complete effectiveness. It is the latter which makes up for the weakness in title. Belligerent occupation presents an illuminating example of this relation of inverse proportion. Belligerent occupation is thus the classical case in which the requirement of effectiveness as a condition of validity of a legal order is abandoned." Krystyna Marek, *Identity and Continuity of States in Public International Law*, 2nd ed., (Librairie Droz 1968),102.

[12] James Crawford, *The Creation of States in International Law*, 2nd ed., (Oxford Press 2006), 701. A presumption is a rule of law where the finding of a basic fact will give rise to the existence of a presumed fact, until it is rebutted.

[13] Matthew Craven, Professor of International Law, Dean, University of London, SOAS, authored a legal opinion for the acting Hawaiian Government concerning the continuity of the Hawaiian Kingdom, and the United States' failure to properly extinguish the Hawaiian State under international law (12 July

2002). Reprinted at *Hawaiian Journal of Law & Politics* 1(Summer 2004): 508-544, 512.

[14] 31 U.S. Stat. 141.

[15] *Id.*

[16] United States Bureau of the Census, *General characteristics—Hawai'i*, 18 (U.S. Government Printing Office 1952).

[17] *Id.*

[18] Convention Relative to the Protection of Civilian Persons in Time of War, Aug. 12, 1949, 6 UST 3516, 75 UNTS 287.

[19] Benvenisti, 140.

[20] *Id.*

[21] *Transmission of Information under Article 73(e) of the Charter*, December 14, 1946, United Nations General Assembly Resolution 66(I).

[22] *Kahawaiola'a v. Norton*, 386 F.3d 1271, at 1282 (9th Cir. 2004).

[23] *Principles which should guide Members in determining whether or not an obligation exists to transmit the information called for under Article 73 (e) of the Charter*, December 15, 1960, United Nations Resolution 1541 (XV).

[24] Tom Coffman, *Nation Within: The Story of America's Annexation of the Nation of Hawai'i* (Tom Coffman/Epicenter 1999), 322.

[25] "Transcript of the Senate Secret Session on Seizure of the Hawaiian Islands, May 31, 1898," *Hawaiian Journal of Law & Politics* 1 (Summer 2004): 230-284, 280.

[26] Act 86 (H.B. No. 425), Territory of Hawai'i, 26 April 1923.

[27] *Cessation of the transmission of information under Article 73(e) of the Charter: communication from the Government of the United States of America*, September 24, 1959, United Nations Document A/4226, 100.

[28] 73 U.S. Stat. 4.

[29] Cessation of Info., 100.

[30] *Id.*

[31] Douglas Kmiec, "Legal Issues Raised by Proposed Presidential Proclamation To Extend the Territorial Sea," *Opinions of the Office of Legal Counsel of the U.S. Department of Justice* 12 (1988): 238-263, 252.

[32] Lawrence H. Fuchs, *Hawai'i Pono: A Social History*, (Harcourt, Brace & World 1961), 68.

[33] Momi Kamahele, "'Ilio'ulaokalani: Defending Native Hawaiian Culture," *Ameraisa Journal* 26(2) (2000): 38-65, 40.

[34] Sam L. No'eau Warner, "The Movement to Revitalize Hawaiian Language and Culture," in *The Green Book of Language Revitalization in Practice*, edited by Leanne Hinton and Ken Hale, (Academic Press 2001), 133.

[35] Michael Dudley & Keoni Agard, *A Call for Hawaiian Sovereignty* (Nā Kāne O Ka Malo Press 1993), 107.

[36] John Dominis Holt, *On Being Hawaiian*, 4th ed. (Ku Pa'a 1995), 7.

[37] Coffman, xii.

[38] *Id.*

[39] Tom Coffman, *Catch a Wave: A Case Study of Hawai'i's New Politics* (University of Hawai'i Press 1973), 1.

[40] Coffman, *Nation Within*, xxii.

[41] Holt, 7.

[42] Gavan Daws, *Shoal of Time* (University of Hawai'i Press 1974), 291.

[43] Noenoe Silva, *Aloha Betrayed: Native Hawaiian Resistance to American Colonialism* (Duke Press 2004), 3.

[44] James Anaya, *Indigenous Peoples in International Law* (Oxford University Press 2000), 22.

[45] 43 U.S.C.S §1601.

[46] *Hawaiians: Organizing Our People*, a pamphlet produced by the students in "ES221—The Hawaiians" in the Ethnic Studies Program at the University of Hawai'i's, at Manoa, 37 (University of Hawai'i 1974).

[47] David Keanu Sai, "American Occupation of the Hawaiian State," 1 *Hawaiian Journal of Law & Politics* (Summer 2004): 46-81, 47.

[48] Linda Tuhiwai Smith, *Decolonizing Methodologies: Research and Indigenous Peoples* (Zed Books Ltd. 1999), 113.

[49] Dudley & Agard, 109.

[50] *Id.,* 113.

[51] *Id.*

[52] Article XII, section 5 of the State of Hawai'i Constitution states: "There is hereby established an Office of Hawaiian Affairs. The Office of Hawaiian Affairs shall hold title to all the real and personal property now or hereafter set aside or conveyed to it which shall be held in trust for native Hawaiians and Hawaiians. There shall be a board of trustees for the Office of Hawaiian Affairs elected by qualified voters who are Hawaiians, as provided by law. The board members shall be Hawaiians. There shall be not less than nine members of the board of trustees; provided that each of the following Islands have one representative: O'ahu, Kaua'i, Maui, Moloka'i and Hawai'i. The board shall select a chairperson from its members."

[53] Native Hawaiian Data Book 1996, Office of Hawaiian Affairs, Planning and Research Office, Appendix.

[54] Since 2000, the Office of Hawaiian Affairs has been challenged on federal constitutional grounds that the program is race-based and violates the equal protection clause of the U.S. constitution. These cases included *Rice v. Cayetano*, 528 U.S. 495 (2000), *Carroll v. Nakatani (Barrett v. State of Hawai'i)*, 188 F. Supp. 2d 1219 (D. Haw. 2001), *Arakaki v. State of Hawai'i*, 314 F.3d 1091 (9th Cir. 2002), and *Arakaki v. Lingle*, 305 F. Supp. 2d 1161 (D. Haw. 2004). Of these cases, only *Rice v. Cayetano* and *Arakaki v. State of Hawai'i* were successful in removing a racial qualification of native Hawaiian ancestry necessary for voting and running for office as a trustee of the Office of Hawaiian Affairs. The federal court dismissed the other two cases after determining that the plaintiffs did not have standing to sue the State of Hawai'i.

[55] Duncan Ivison, Paul Patton & Will Sanders, *Political Theory and the Rights of Indigenous Peoples* (Cambridge University Press 2000), 89.

[56] Haunani-Kay Trask, "Settlers of Color and 'Immigrant' Hegemony: 'Locals' in Hawai'i," *Amerasia* 26(2) (2000): 1-24, 17.

[57] Noel Kent, *Hawai'i: Islands under the Influence* (University of Hawai'i Press 1993), 198.

[58] Jeff J. Corntassel & Tomas Hopkins Primeau, "Indigenous 'Sovereignty' and International Law: Revised Strategies for Pursuing 'Self-Determination,'" *Human Rights Quarterly* 17(2) (1995): 343-365, 347.

[59] Andrew H. Walsh, *Historical Memorandum on the Hawaiian Revolution of 1893 for the UCC's Sovereignty Project* (30 November 1992), 24.

[60] Eric Yamamoto, *Interracial Justice: Conflict & Reconciliation in Post-Civil Rights America* (New York University Press 1999), 215.

[61] *Id.,* 52.

[62] Sally Merry, *Colonizing Hawai'i: The Cultural Power of Law* (Princeton University Press 2000); Jonathan Osorio, *Dismembering Lahui: A History of the Hawaiian Nation to 1887* (University of Hawai'i Press 2002); Robert Stauffer, *Kahana: How the Land Was Lost* (University of Hawai'i Press 2004).

[63] U.S. Public Law 103-150 (107 Stat. 1510).

[64] *Id.,* 1513.

[65] S. 381, §1(19), 111th Congress (2009).

[66] Rupert Emerson, "Self-Determination," *American Journal of International Law* 65(3) (July 1971): 459-475, 463.

[67] *Id.*

[68] *Id.*

[69] *"U.S. National Security Council, Position on Indigenous Peoples,"* January 18, 2001.

[70] *Id.*

[71] Milton J. Esman, "Ethnic Pluralism and International Relations," *Canadian Review of Studies in Nationalism* 17(1-2) (1990): 83-93, 88.

[72] *Black's Law Dictionary*, 6th ed. (West Publishing Company 1990), 265.

[73] Albert Galloway Keller, *Colonization: A Study of the Founding of New Societies* (Ginn & Company 1908), 1.

[74] *Id.*, 2.

[75] Slavoj Zizek, *Interrogating the Real* (Continuum 2005), 92.

[76] *Id. Erstaz* is German for an imitation or substitute.

[77] Matthew Craven, "Hawai'i, History, and International Law," *Hawaiian Journal of Law and Politics* 1 (Summer 2004): 6-22, 8.

[78] Tom Coffman, *Nation Within: The History of the American Occupation of Hawai'i*, revised edition (Koa Books, 2009).

[79] *Id.*, xvi.

[80] Marek, 80.

[81] *Id.*

[82] *Compiled Laws of the Hawaiian Kingdom* (Hawaiian Gazette 1884), 2.

[83] The American Heritage Dictionary, 2nd College ed. (Houghton Mifflin Company 1982), 857.

[84] Sir William R. Anson, *Principles of the Law of Contract* (Callaghan and Company 1880), 4

[85] John Bouvier, *Bouvier's Law Dictionary and Concise Encyclopedia*, 8th ed., vol. 1 (West Publishing Company 1914), 179.

[86] *Id.*

[87] *Penal Code of the Hawaiian Islands*, (Government Press 1869), 8.

[88] *Id.*

[89] von Glahn, *The Occupation of Enemy Territory*, 56.

[90] Henry Wager Halleck, *International Law* (D.Van Nostrand 1861), 791.

[91] von Glahn, *Law Among Nations*, 777.

[92] David J. Hill, "The Rights of the Civil Population in Territory Occupied by a Belligerent," *The American Journal of International Law* 11(1) (1917): 133-137, 134.

[93] Benvenisti, *The International Law of Occupation* (Princeton University Press 1993), 14.

[94] *Ho Tung and Co. v. The United States*, 42 Ct. Cls. 213, 227-228 (1907).

[95] von Glahn, *The Occupation of Enemy Territory*, 97.

[96] William E. Birkhimer, *Military Government and Martial Law* (James J. Chapman 1892), 21.

[97] Benvenisti, 19.

[98] "United States Army and Navy Manual of Military Government and Civil Affairs," *U.S. Army Field Manual* 27-5, para. 3 (December 22, 1843)

[99] Thomas M. Cooley, *The General Principles of Constitutional Law in the United States of America* (Little, Brown, and Company 1898), 190.

[100] Ernst Feilchenfeld, *The International Economic Law of Belligerent Occupation* (Carnegie Endowment for International Peace 1942), 145.

[101] Stefan Talmon, "Who is a Legitimate Government in Exile? Towards Normative Criteria for Governmental Legitimacy in International Law," *The Reality of International Law: Essays in Honour of Ian*

Brownlie, Guy S. Goodwin-Gill and Stephan Talmon, ed.'s (Clarendon Press 1999), 522.

[102] Lassa Oppenheim, *International Law*, 7th ed., vol. 2 (Longmans 1952), 218.

[103] Malcolm Nathan Shaw, *International Law*, 5th ed. (Cambridge University Press 2003), 390.

[104] *Id.*, 392.

[105] Marek, 110.

[106] 19 League of Nations Official Journal 341 (1938).

[107] Marek, 115.

[108] *Id.*, 113.

[109] "The Law of Land Warfare", *U.S. Army Field Manual* 27-10 §366 (July 1956).

[110] United States House of Representatives, 53rd Congress, Executive Documents on Affairs in Hawai'i: 1894-95, (Government Printing Office 1895), 453.

[111] 107 U.S. Stat. 1510. Reprinted at *Hawaiian Journal of Law and Politics* 1 (Summer 2004): 290.

[112] Benvenisti, 212.

[113] Public Law 96-565.

[114] Native Hawaiian Studies Commission, "Report on the culture, needs and concerns of Native Hawaiians, vol. 1," *Pursuant to Public Law* 96-565, Title III (1983), 27.

[115] *Id.*, 346.

[116] *Id.*, 347.

[117] Craven, *Hawai'i, History, and International Law*, 8.

[118] George B. Davis, *The Elements of International Law* (Harper & Brothers 1903), 31.

[119] *Id.*

[120] Umozurike Oji Umozurike, *Self-Determination in International Law* (Archon 1972), 4.

[121] Andrew Schaap, *Political Reconciliation* (Routledge 2005), 13.

[122] John Torpey, *Politics and the Past: On Repairing Historical Injustices* (Rowman & Littlefield 2003), 25.

[123] Mark R. Amstutz, *The Healing of Nations: The Promise and Limits of Political Forgiveness* (Rowman & Littlefield Publishers 2005), 27.

[124] Dinah Shelton, "Righting Wrongs: Reparations in the Articles of State Responsibility," *American Journal of International Law* 96(4) (Oct., 2003): 833-856, 836.

[125] *Chorzow Factory* (Germany v. Poland), Indemnity, 1928 PCIJ (ser. A), no. 17, 47.

[126] von Glahn, *Occupation of Enemy Territory*, 94.

[127] Ian Brownlie, *Principles of Public International Law*, 4th ed. (Clarendon Press 1990), 287.

[128] Ian Brownlie, *System of the Law of Nations: State Responsibility*, Part I (Oxford University Press 1983), 211.

[129] *Chorzow Factory* case, 29.

[130] Gerald Fitzmaurice, *The Law and Procedure of the International Court of Justice* (Grotius 1986), 6.

[131] Restatement (Third) of the Foreign Relations Law of the United States, §901 (1987).

[132] James Crawford, *The International Law Commission's Articles on State Responsibility: Introduction, Text and Commentaries* (Cambridge University Press 2002), 215.

[133] *Id.*, 1.

[134] Brownlie, *System of the Law of Nations*, 30.

[135] Crawford, *International Law Commission*, 58.

[136] *Id.*, 59. See also G.A. Res. 59/35 of December 2, 2004.

[137] *Id.* See also Fourth Report, A/CN.4/517, para. 26.

[138] David D. Caron, "The ILC Articles on State Responsibility: The Paradoxical Relationship Between Form and Authority," *American Journal of International Law* 96 (2002): 857-873, 867; see also Brownlie,

System of the Law of Nations, 25.

[139] James Crawford, "Fourth Report on State Responsibility," U.N. Doc. A/CN. 4/517, para. 22 (2001).

[140] Caron, 838.

[141] Lauri Malksoo, "State Responsibility and the Challenge of the Realist Paradigm: The Demand of Baltic Victims of Soviet Mass Repressions for Compensation from Russia," *Baltic Yearbook of International Law* 3 (2003): 57-76, 58.

[142] Shelton, 842.

[143] *Id.*

[144] *Id.*, 856.

[145] John R. Crook, "The United Nations Compensation Commission—A New Structure to Enforce State Responsibility," *American Journal of International Law* 87(1) (1993): 144-157, 144.

[146] The United Nations established a website for the *United Nations Compensation Commission*. The website is an excellent resource of information regarding the claims by states, individuals and businesses against Iraq as well as selected publications. <http://www2.unog.ch/uncc/>.

[147] Crawford, *International Law Commission*, 81.

[148] Mavrommatis Palestine Concession case, PCIJ, Ser. A, no. 2, 11.

[149] U.N. Charter, Article 33.

[150] According to Brownlie, a "state presenting an international claim to another state, either in diplomatic exchanges or before an international tribunal, has to establish its qualifications for making the claim, and the continuing viability of the claim itself, before the merits of the claim come into question." Brownlie, *Public International Law*, 477.

[151] Article 69 of the 1969 Vienna Convention on the Law of Treaties defines a "peremptory norm or general international law [as] a norm accepted and recognized by the international community of States as a whole as a norm from which no derogation is permitted and which can be modified only by a subsequent norm of general international law having the same character." See Vienna Convention on the Law of Treaties (1969), United Nations, *Treaty Series*, vol. 1155, 331.

[152] Crawford, *International Law Commission*, 162.

SELECTED BIBLIOGRAPHY

Addleman, William, *History of the United States Army in Hawai'i*, 1849-1939, (Hawai'i War Records Depository, Hamilton Library, University of Hawai'i, Manoa).

American Journal of International Law, "Judicial Decisions Involving Questions of International Law," 21 (4) (Oct., 1927): 777-811.

Amstutz, Mark R., *The Healing of Nations: The Promise and Limits of Political Forgiveness* (Rowman & Littlefield Publishers 2005).

Anson, Sir William R., *Principles of the Law of Contract* (Callaghan and Company 1880).

Alexander, W.D., "A Brief History of Land Titles in the Hawaiian Kingdom," *Interior Department, Appendix to Surveyor General's Report to the 1882 Hawaiian Legislature*.

___. *A Brief History of the Hawaiian People* (American Book Company 1891).

Anaya, James, *Indigenous Peoples in International Law* (Oxford University Press 2000).

Bailey, T.A., "The United States and Hawai'i During the Spanish-American War," *The American Historical Review* 36(3) (April 1931): 552-560.

Benvenisti, Eyal, *The International Law of Occupation* (Princeton University Press 1993).

Birkhimer, William E., *Military Government and Martial Law* (James J. Chapman 1892).

Blackstone, William, *Commentaries of the Laws of England*, vol. 4 (Chicago: The University of Chicago Press 1979).

Born, Gary, *International Civil Litigation in United States Courts*, 3rd ed., (Kluwer Law International 1996).

Brown, Arthur, *A Compendious View of the Civil Law, and of the Law of the Admiralty*, 2nd ed. (G. Woodfall 1802).

Brownlie, Ian, *System of the Law of Nations: State Responsibility*, Part I (Oxford University Press 1983).

___. *Principles of Public International Law*, 4th ed. (Clarendon Press 1990).

Caron, David D., "The ILC Articles on State Responsibility: The Paradoxical Relationship Between Form and Authority," *American Journal of International Law* 96 (2002): 857-873.

Carter, Bryum, *The Office of Prime Minister* (Princeton University Press, 1956).

Coffman, Tom, *Catch a Wave: A Case Study of Hawai'i's New Politics* (University of Hawai'i Press 1973).

___. Nation Within: *The Story of America's Annexation of the Nation of Hawai'i* (Tom Coffman/Epicenter 1999).

Cooley, Thomas M., *The General Principles of Constitutional in the United States of America* (Little, Brown, and Company 1898).

Corntassel, Jeff J. & Primeau, Tomas Hopkins, "Indigenous 'Sovereignty' and International Law: Revised Strategies for Pursuing 'Self-Determination,'" *Human Rights Quarterly* 17(2) (1995): 343-365.

Corwin, Edward S., "Constitution v. Constitutional Theory," *The American Political Science Review* 19(2) (1925): 290-304.

Craven, Matthew, "Hawai'i, History, and International Law," *Hawaiian Journal of Law and Politics* 1 (Summer 2004): 6-22.

___. "Legal Opinion (Portion) by Dr. Matthew Craven Concerning the Continuity of the Hawaiian State, July 12, 2002" *Hawaiian Journal of Law and Politics* 1 (Summer 2004): 508-544.

Crawford, James, *The International Law Commission's Articles on State Responsibility: Introduction, Text and Commentaries* (Cambridge University Press 2002).

___. *The Creation of States in International Law*, 2nd ed., (Oxford Press 2006).

Crook, John R., "The United Nations Compensation Commission—A New Structure to Enforce State Responsibility," *American Journal of International Law* 87(1) (1993): 144-157.

Dudley, Michael & Agard, Keoni, *A Call for Hawaiian Sovereignty* (Nā Kāne O Ka Malo Press 1993).

Davis, George B., *The Elements of International Law* (Harper & Brothers 1903).

Daws, Gavan, *Shoal of Time* (University of Hawai'i Press 1974).

Dibble, Sheldon, *A History of the Sandwich Islands* (Thomas G. Thrum, Publisher 1909).

Dumberry, Patrick, "The Hawaiian Kingdom Arbitration Case and the Unsettled Question of the Hawaiian Kingdom's Claim to Continue as an Independent State under International Law," *Chinese Journal of International Law* 1(1)(2002): 655-684.

Emerson, Rupert, "Self-Determination," *American Journal of International Law* 65(3) (July 1971): 459-475.

Esman, Milton J., "Ethnic Pluralism and International Relations," *Canadian Review of Studies in Nationalism* 17(1-2) (1990): 83-93.

Feilchenfeld, Ernst, *The International Economic Law of Belligerent Occupation* (Carnegie Endowment for International Peace 1942).

Fitzmaurice, Gerald, *The Law and Procedure of the International Court of Justice* (Grotius 1986).

Fornander, Abraham, *Ancient History of the Hawaiian People to the Times of Kamehameha I* (Mutual Publishing 1996).

Frear, Walter, "The Evolution of the Hawaiian Judiciary," *Papers of the Hawaiian Historical Society* (June 29, 1894).

___. "Hawaiian Statute Law," *Thirteenth Annual Report of the Hawaiian Historical Society* (Hawaiian Gazette Co., Ltd. 1906).

Fuller, L.L., "Legal Fictions," *Illinois Law Review* 25 (Dec. 1930): 363-399.

Fuchs, Lawrence H., *Hawai'i Pono: A Social History*, (Harcourt, Brace & World 1961).

Hackler, Rhoda E.A., "Alliance or Cession? Missing Letter from Kamehameha I to King George III of England Casts Light on 1794 Agreement," 20 *The Hawaiian Journal of History* (1986): 1-12.

Halleck, Henry Wager, *International Law* (D.Van Nostrand 1861).

Hawaiian Almanac and Annual, "The Hawaiian Flag," (Thos. G. Thrum 1880).

___. "Hawaiian Register and Directory for 1893," (Thos. G. Thrum 1892).

___. "John Young: Companion of Kamehameha, a Brief Sketch of His Life in Hawai'i," (Thos. G. Thrum 1910).

___. "Early Constitution of the Judiciary of the Hawaiian Islands, by A.F. Judd" (Thos. G. Thrum 1888).

Hawaiian Journal of Law and Politics, "1849 Treaty of Friendship, Commerce and Navigation," 1 (Summer 2004): 115-125.

___. "1875 Treaty of Reciprocity," 1 (Summer 2004): 126-128.

___. "1883 Postal Convention Concerning Money Orders," 1 (Summer 2004): 129-133.

___. "1884 Supplementary Convention to the 1875 Treaty of Reciprocity," 1 (Summer 2004): 134-135.

___. "Transcript of the Senate Secret Session on Seizure of the Hawaiian Islands, May 31, 1898," 1 (Summer 2004): 230-284, 280.

Hill, David J., "The Rights of the Civil Population in Territory Occupied by a Belligerent," *The American Journal of International Law* 11(1) (1917): 133-137.

Holt, John Dominis, *On Being Hawaiian*, 4th ed. (Ku Pa'a 1995).

Ivison, Duncan, Patton, Paul & Sanders, Will, *Political Theory and the Rights of Indigenous Peoples* (Cambridge University Press 2000).

Jarves, James Jackson, *History of the Hawaiian Islands*, 3rd ed. (Charles Edwin Hitchcock 1847).

Kamahele, Momi, "'Ilio'ulaokalani: Defending Native Hawaiian Culture," *Ameraisa Journal* 26(2) (2000): 38-65.

Kamakau, Samuel Mānaiakalani, *Ka Po'e Kahiko*: The People of Old (The Bishop Museum Press 1964).

___. *Ruling Chiefs of Hawai'i* (Kamehameha Schools Press 1992).

Keith, A.B., *The King and the Imperial Crown* (Longman, Green and Co., 1936).

Keller, Albert Galloway, *Colonization: A Study of the Founding of New Societies* (Ginn & Company 1908).

Kent, Noel, *Hawai'i: Islands under the Influence* (University of Hawai'i Press 1993).

Kmiec, Douglas, "Legal Issues Raised by Proposed Presidential Proclamation To Extend the Territorial Sea," *Opinions of the Office of Legal Counsel of the U.S. Department of Justice* 12 (1988): 238-263.

Kuykendall, Ralph S., The Hawaiian Kingdom: 1778-1854, Foundation and Transformation, vol. 1 (University of Hawai'i Press 1938).

___. *The Hawaiian Kingdom: 1874-1893, The Kalakaua Dynasty*, vol. III (University of Hawai'i Press 1967).

Lili'uokalani, *Hawai'i's Story by Hawai'i's Queen* (Charles E. Tuttle Co., Inc. 1964).

Lind, Ian, "Ring of Steel: Notes on the Militarization of Hawai'i," *Social Process in Hawai'i* 31 (1984-85): 25-47.

Lydecker, Robert C., *Roster Legislatures of Hawai'i, 1841-1918* (The Hawaiian Gazette Co., Ltd. 1918).

Maitland, F.W., *The Constitutional History of England* (University Press 1926).

Malksoo, Lauri, "State Responsibility and the Challenge of the Realist Paradigm: The Demand of Baltic Victims of Soviet Mass Repressions for Compensation from Russia," *Baltic Yearbook of International Law* 3 (2003): 57-76.

Malo, David, *Hawaiian Antiquities* (Bishop Museum 1951).

Marek, Krystyna, *Identity and Continuity of States in Public International Law*, 2nd ed., (Librairie Droz 1968).

Merry, Sally, *Colonizing Hawai'i: The Cultural Power of Law* (Princeton University Press 2000).

Moore, John Basset, *Digest of International Law*, Vol. I (Government Printing Office 1906).

Mykkanen, Juri, *Inventing Politics: A New Political Anthropology of the Hawaiian Kingdom*, (University of Hawai'i Press 2003).

Oppenheim, Lassa, *International Law*, 3rd ed., (Longmans, Green & Co. 1920).

Oppenheim, Lassa, *International Law*, 7th ed., vol. 2 (Longmans 1952).

Osorio, Jonathon, *Dismembering Lahui: A History of the Hawaiian Nation to 1887* (University of Hawai'i Press 2002).

Richards, William, "William Richard's Report to the Sandwich Islands Mission on His First Year In Government Service, 1838-1839," *Fifty-first Annual Report of the Hawaiian Historical Society for the Year 1942* (Hawaiian Printing Company, Limited, 1943).

___. *No ke Kālai'āina* (Lahaina: Lahainaluna High School Press, 1840).

___. *Translation of the Constitution and Laws of the Hawaiian Islands, established in the reign of Kamehameha III* (Lahainaluna, 1842).

Sagan, Eli, *At the Dawn of Tyranny: The Origins of Individualism, Political Oppression, and the State* (Alfred A. Knopf 1985).

Sai, David Keanu, "American Occupation of the Hawaiian State," 1 *Hawaiian Journal of Law & Politics* (Summer 2004): 46-81.

___. "A Slippery Path Towards Hawaiian Indigeneity," 10 *Journal of Law and Social Challenges* (Fall 2008): 68-133.

Schaap, Andrew, *Political Reconciliation* (Routledge 2005).

Shaw, Malcolm Nathan, *International Law*, 5th ed. (Cambridge University Press 2003).

Scheffer, David J., "Beyond Occupation Law," *American Journal of International Law* 97(4) (October 2003): 842-860.

Shelton, Dinah, "Righting Wrongs: Reparations in the Articles of State Responsibility," *American Journal of International Law* 96(4) (October 2003): 833-856.

Schroeder, Christopher, "Validity of Congressional-Executive Agreements that Substantially Modify the United States' obligations Under an Existing Treaty," *Opinions of the Office of Legal Counsel of the U.S. Department of Justice* 20 (1996): 389-401.

Silva, Noenoe, *Aloha Betrayed: Native Hawaiian Resistance to American Colonialism* (Duke University Press 2004).

Smith, Linda Tuhiwai, *Decolonizing Methodologies: Research and Indigenous Peoples* (Zed Books Ltd. 1999).

Stauffer, Robert, *Kahana: How the Land Was Lost* (University of Hawai'i Press 2004).

Stewart, C.S., *A Visit to the South Seas, in the U.S. Ship Vincennes, during the years 1829 and 1830*, (New York: Sleight & Robinson, 1831).

Talmon, Stefan, "Who is a Legitimate Government in Exile? Towards Normative Criteria for Governmental Legitimacy in International Law," *The Reality of International Law: Essays in Honour of Ian Brownlie*, Guy S. Goodwin-Gill and Stephan Talmon, ed.'s (Clarendon Press 1999).

Tate, Merze, *The United States and the Hawaiian Kingdom* (Greenwood Press 1980).

Thurston, Lorrin A., *The Fundamental Law of Hawai'i* (The Hawaiian Gazette Co., Ltd. 1904).

Torpey, John, *Politics and the Past: On Repairing Historical Injustices* (Rowman & Littlefield 2003).

Trask, Haunani-Kay, "Settlers of Color and 'Immigrant' Hegemony: 'Locals' in Hawai'i," *Amerasia* 26(2) (2000): 1-24.

Umozurike, Umozurike Oji, Self-Determination in International Law (Archon 1972).

United States House of Representatives, 53rd Congress, Executive Documents on Affairs in Hawaii: 1894-95 (Government Printing Office 1895).

Vancouver, George, *Voyage of Discovery to the North Pacific Ocean and the round the World*, vol. 3 (Da Capo Press 1967).

von Glahn, Gehard, *The Occupation of Enemy Territory: A Commentary on the Law and Practice of Belligerent Occupation* (University of Minnesota Press 1957).

___. *Law Among Nations*, 6th ed. (Maxwell Macmillan Canada, Inc. 1992).

Walker, David M., *The Oxford Companion to Law* (Clarendon Press 1980).

Walsh, Andrew H., *Historical Memorandum on the Hawaiian Revolution of 1893 for the UCC's Sovereignty Project* (30 November 1992).

Warner, Sam L. No'eau, "The Movement to Revitalize Hawaiian Language and Culture," in *The Green Book of Language Revitalization in Practice*, edited by Leanne Hinton and Ken Hale, (Academic Press 2001).

Westervelt, W.D., "Hawaiian Printed Laws Before the Constitution," *Sixteenth Annual Report of the Hawaiian Historical Society and Papers, December 31, 1908* (Hawaiian Gazette Co., Ltd. 1909).

Willoughby, Westel, *The Constitutional Law of the United States*, 2nd ed., (Baker, Voorhis 1929).

Yack, Bernard, "The Rationality of Hegel's Concept of Monarchy," *The American Political Science Review* 74(3) (1980): 709-720.

Yamamoto, Eric, *Interracial Justice: Conflict & Reconciliation in Post-Civil Rights America* (New York University Press 1999).

Zizek, Slavoj, *Interrogating the Real* (Continuum 2005).

COURT CASES

HAWAIIAN KINGDOM

In the Matter of the Estate of His Majesty Kamehameha IV, 3 Hawai'i 715 (1864).

Rex v. Joseph Booth, 3 Hawai'i 616 (1863).

UNITED STATES OF AMERICA

Arakaki v. State of Hawai'i, 314 F.3d 1091 (9th Cir. 2002).

Arakaki v. Lingle, 305 F. Supp. 2d 1161 (D. Haw. 2004).

Carroll v. Nakatani (*Barrett v. State of Hawai'i*), 188 F. Supp. 2d 1219 (D. Haw. 2001).

Ex parte Milligan, 71 U.S. 2 (1866).

Ho Tung and Co. v. The United States, 42 Ct. Cls. 213, 227-228 (1907).

Kahawaiola'a v. Norton, 386 F.3d 1271, at 1282 (9th Cir. 2004).

Rice v. Cayetano, 528 U.S. 495 (2000).

Rose v. Himely, 8 U.S. 241, 279 (1807).

Smythe v. Fiske, 90 U.S. (23 Wall.) 374 (1874).

Territory of Hawai'i v. Mankichi, 190 U.S. 197, 212 (1903).

The Apollon, 22 U.S. 362, 370 (1824).

INTERNATIONAL

Chorzow Factory (Germany v. Poland), Indemnity, 1928 PCIJ (ser. A), no. 17

GLOSSARY

Aboriginal—A people first to arrive in a particular region. The native population of the Hawaiian Islands is called aboriginal Hawaiians. In the Hawaiian language, a full-blooded aboriginal Hawaiian is kanaka maoli, and a part aboriginal Hawaiian is hapa haole. As stated in the last will and testament of Princess Bernice Pauahi Bishop (Oct. 31, 1883), "I direct may trustees…to devote a portion of each years income to the support and education of orphans, and others in indigent circumstances, giving the preference to Hawaiians of pure or part aboriginal blood."

Agrarian—Relating to land, land tenure, or the division of landed property: agrarian laws; pertaining to the advancement of agricultural groups: an agrarian movement.

Agreement of restoration (executive agreement)—An agreement entered into between Queen Liliʻuokalani and President Grover Cleveland settling the illegal overthrow of the Hawaiian Kingdom government by the forces of the United States that aided and supported an uprising of a minority group of people on January 17th 1893. Under the agreement, the President would restore the Hawaiian Kingdom government as it stood on the day of the illegally landing of U.S. troops on January 16th 1893, reassign the executive power to the Queen, and the Queen thereafter to grant amnesty to the insurgents. Under international law, the Agreement of restoration, is a treaty, and under United States law, it is considered a sole executive agreement that does not require ratification from the U.S. Senate or approval of Congress to have the force and effect of a treaty.

Alien—A citizen or subject of a foreign country or state residing within the territory of the Hawaiian Kingdom.

Aliʻi—Chief, chiefess, officer, ruler, monarch, peer, headman, noble, aristocrat, king, queen, commander; royal, regal, aristocrat, kingly; to rule or act as a chief, govern, reign; to become a chief.

Amnesty—A pardon for an offense or conviction. In the United States amnesty can be granted before conviction, but in the Hawaiian Kingdom amnesty can only be given after the conviction. According to article 27 of the Hawaiian Constitution, "The King, by and with the advice of His Privy Council, has the power to grant reprieves and pardons, after conviction, for all offenses, except in cases of impeachment."

Annexation—A formal act whereby a country or state declares its sovereignty over territory outside its own territory. Unlike cession, whereby territory is granted or conveyed through treaty, annexation is a unilateral act.

Bicameral legislature—A legislative body with two houses, i.e. House of Nobles and the House of Representatives.

Bunting—A type of lightweight fabric used to make ribbons and flags.

Cabinet Council—An executive body of ministers of a constitutional monarchy. According to article 42 of the Hawaiian Constitution, "The King's Cabinet shall consist of the Minister of Foreign Affairs, the Minister of the Interior, the Minister of Finance, and the Attorney General of the Kingdom, and these shall be His Majesty's Special Advisers in the Executive affairs of the Kingdom; and they shall be ex officio Members of His Majesty's Privy Council of State. They shall be appointed and commissioned by the King, and hold office during His Majesty's pleasure, subject to impeachment. No act of the King shall have any effect unless it be countersigned by a Minister, who by that signature makes himself responsible."

Cession (cede)—The process by which a sovereign state or nation conveys territory to another sovereign state. The evidence of the transfer of territory is a treaty or bi-lateral agreement between the state or nation, as grantor, and a state, as grantee.

Civil Code—An organized collection of civil laws for a society published in book form that is intended for easy access by the populace.

Civil law—A legal system inspired by Roman law that is written into a collection, codified, and, unlike the common law, it does not include judge-made law through court decisions or case law.

Colony— A dependent political community, consisting of a number of citizens of the same country who have emigrated therefrom to people another, and remain subject to the mother country. Territory attached to another nation, known as the mother country, with political and economic ties; e.g. possessions or dependencies of the British Crown (e.g. thirteen original colonies of the United States).

Colonization—Colonization is the building and maintaining of colonies in one territory by people from another country or state. It is the process, by which sovereignty over the territory of a colony is claimed by the mother country or state, and is exercised and controlled by the nationals of the colonizing country or state. Though colonization there is an unequal relationship between the colonizer and the native populations that reside within its colonial territory. These native populations are referred to as indigenous peoples and form the basis of the 2007 United Nations Declaration on the Rights of Indigenous Peoples.

Comity—Also called comity of nations. Courtesy between nations, as in respect shown by one country for the laws, judicial decisions, and institutions of another

Common law—A legal system that is solely developed by judges through court decisions, rather than by statutes enacted by the legislature. Court decisions, as common law, sets precedence in other cases, which provides predictability in the courts.

Congressional Authority—Under the separation of powers doctrine, the U.S. Congress is vested with legislative power under article I of the U.S. Constitution to enact laws over U.S. territory, called territorial sovereignty, and over U.S. citizens abroad, called personal supremacy. Congressional authority has no force beyond U.S. territory, except over U.S. citizens.

Constitution—The organic and fundamental law of a nation or state, which may be written or unwritten, establishing the character and conception of its government, laying the basic principles to which its internal life is to be conformed, organizing the government, and regulating, distributing, and limiting the functions of its different departments, and prescribing the extent and manner of the exercise of sovereign powers.

Constitutionalism—A political theory that government should be limited in its powers under a written constitution, and that its authority is based and depends on the rule of law as opposed to rule by the arbitrary judgment of government officials. The separation of powers doctrine is the cornerstone of constitutionalism.

Cooperative capitalism—A form of capitalism promoted by Professor Francis Waylands that was cooperative in nature. Although Wayland's cooperative capitalism still promoted an economic and political system whereby a country's trade and industry are controlled by private ownership for profit, it was infused with Christian values and morality amongst the private owners as well as government. Waylands' theory became the basis of the Hawaiian Kingdom's political economy.

Customary law—As distinguished from laws being developed at the top, customary law may have been introduced from the top but it develops at the bottom through widespread acceptance, custom, and usage.

De-colonization—De-colonization is the political process by which a non-self-governing territory under the sovereignty of the colonizing state or country becomes self-governing. According to the United Nations Resolution 1541 (XV), *Principles which should guide Members in determining whether or not an obligation exists to transmit the information called for under Article 73 e of the Charter*, "A Non-Self-Governing Territory can be said to have reached a full measure of self-government by: (a) Emergence as a sovereign independent State; (b) Free association with an independent State; or (c) Integration with an independent State."

De facto—In fact.

De jure—In law.

De-occupation—De-occupation is the political process by which the occupation of a sovereign independent state comes to an end. This will take place when the control over governance of the territory is transferred from the occupying military government of the occupying state or country to the restored or returning legitimate government of the occupied state or country. De-occupation is limited to restoration of the legitimate government and does not affect the sovereignty of the state or country, its national population, its territorial boundaries, nor its legal order as would the process of decolonization.

English Colours—English flags.

Erstaz philosophy—German for an imitation or substitute philosophy.

Executive power—The power of a branch of government to execute and administer law. According to article 31 of the Hawaiian Constitution, "To the King belongs the Executive power."

Federal system—A form of government in which sovereign power is divided between a central or national authority and a number of sub-political units.

Fee-simple—A type of estate granted to a person and his heirs and successors without limitation or condition, but subject to the laws of the country that issued the title.

Feudal—A set of legal and military customs in medieval Europe that provided a set of reciprocal legal and military obligations among the warrior nobility based upon the holding of land. Under a feudal system, absolute ownership was vested in the King, and use of the land granted to Lords and Vassals under certain conditions of allegiance and military service. Feudal arose out of its root word, feodum, which is Latin for estate in land.

Freehold—An estate in land in fee-simple or for life.

Haole—White person, American, Englishman, Caucasian; formerly, any foreigner; foreign introduced, of foreign origin.

Hawaiian—A person that belongs to the Hawaiian Kingdom, such as a national of the Hawaiian Kingdom, irrespective of race, color or creed, called a Hawaiian subject, or property that belongs to the Hawaiian Kingdom, such as territory. In the Hawaiian language, a Hawaiian subject is translated as *kanaka Hawaiʻi* [Hawaiian person], and the Hawaiian Islands as kō Hawaiʻi pae ʻāina [Islands belonging to Hawaiʻi].

Heiau—Pre-christian place of worship, shrine; some heiau were elaborately constructed stone platforms, others simple earth terraces.

Independent State—A state that has absolute and independent legal and political authority over its territory to the exclusion of other states. Once recognized as independent, the state becomes a subject of international law. According to United States common law, an independent State is a people permanently occupying a fixed territory bound together by common law habits and custom into one body politic exercising, through the medium of an organized government, independent sovereignty and control over all persons and things within its boundaries, capable of making war and peace and of entering into international relations with other communities around the globe.

Indigenous—Originating in a particular region as opposed to aboriginal, which is first to arrive in a region. Indigenous was often used to identify plants and animals, and aboriginal was used to identify people.

Indigenous peoples—As a political term coined by the United Nations, indigenous populations comprise the existing descendants of peoples who inhabited the present territory of a country wholly or partially at the time when persons of a different culture or ethnic origin arrived there from other parts of the world, overcame them, by conquest, settlement or other means, reduced them to a non-dominant or colonial condition. According to the 2007 United Nations Declaration on the Rights of Indigenous Peoples, "indigenous peoples have suffered from historic injustices as a result of, inter alia, their colonization and dispossession of their lands, territories and resources, thus preventing them from exercising, in particular, their right to development in accordance with their own needs and interests."

Insurgent—An individual who participates in a rebellion against the lawful authority of a government of a country or state. Insurgency is a criminal act that falls under the crime of treason. According to the Hawaiian Penal Code, "Treason is hereby defined to be any plotting or attempt to dethrone or destroy the King, or the levying of war against the King's government, or the adhering to the enemies thereof giving them aid and comfort, the same being done by a person owing allegiance to this kingdom." The treason statute also states, "An alien, whether his native country be at war or at peace with this kingdom, owes allegiance to this kingdom during his residence therein, and during such residence, is capable of committing treason against this kingdom."

International Law—A law that regulates relations between countries or states, who are called subjects of international law. International law does not regulate private individuals, but rather subjects of international law, which include countries or states and international organizations, e.g. United Nations, Permanent Court of Arbitration, International Court of Justice, International Red Cross. Article 38(1) of the 1946 Statute of the International Court of Justice provides four sources of international law: (a) international conventions, whether general or particular, establishing rules expressly recognized by the contesting states; (b) international custom, as evidence of a general practice accepted as law; (c) the general principles of law recognized by civilized nations; (d) judicial decisions and the teachings of the most highly qualified publicists of the various nations, as subsidiary means for the determination of rules of law.

Joint resolution—A formal expression of the opinion or will of both the House of Representatives and the Senate of the United States.

Judicial power—The power of a branch of government to resolve disputes under the law. According to article 64 of the Hawaiian Constitution, "The Judicial Power of the Kingdom shall be vested in one Supreme Court, and in such Inferior Courts as the Legislature may, from time to time, establish."

Kālai'āina—Political; politics; political economy. Lit., land carving. Kuhina Kālai'āina, Minister of Interior. After the death of a King, all lands formerly distributed to the highest chiefs, who in turn subdivided their lands to their lesser chiefs, down through several descending ranks of chiefs to the commoner class, reverted to the successor of the King for re-distribution. Lands were redistributed based upon allegiance and military service of the chiefs and labor from the commoners. This process of redistribution followed along similar lines of the feudal system of medieval Europe.

Kalo— Taro; a staple of the ancient Hawaiian diet.

Kānāwai— Law, code, rule, statute, act, regulation, ordinance, decree, edict; legal; to obey a law; to be prohibited; to learn from experience.

Kānāwai Akua— God's law.

Kānāwai Kapu Ali'i— Sacred chiefly laws.

Kapu—A law or etiquette that governed ancient society and religion.

Kilokilo—Enchantment, magic, fortune telling; magical.

Konohiki—Headman of an ahupua'a land division under the chief; land or fishing rights under control of the konohiki; such rights are sometimes called konohiki rights.

Kuhina Nui—Powerful officer in the days of the monarchy. Ka'ahumanu was the first to have this title; the position is usually translated as "prime minister" or "premier."

Kūkā'ilimoku—Kamehameha's war image.

Law of Occupation—The laws administered by an occupying government within the territory of an occupied country or state, which includes the national laws of the occupied country or state and the international laws that regulate occupations, *i.e.* 1907 Hague Regulations and the 1949 Geneva Conventions.

Legation—A diplomatic mission in a foreign country ranking below an embassy and headed by a Minister Plenipotentiary. The distinction between a mission and an embassy was dropped after World War II.

Life Estate—A type of estate granted to a person for that person's life and upon the death of that person the estate reverts to the fee-simple owner, who is called the remainderman.

Liliʻuokalani assignment (executive agreement)—Unable to fulfill her constitutional duty to faithfully execute Hawaiian Kingdom law, Queen Liliʻuokalani was forced to temporarily assign her executive power to the President of the United States on January 17th 1893 under threat of war. The Liliʻuokalani assignment mandates the President to temporarily administer Hawaiian Kingdom law as the Queen would under her constitutional authority. According to article 31 of the Hawaiian Constitution, "To the King belongs the Executive power." The Queen's assignment, under protest, did not relinquish the Hawaiian Kingdom, but only the executive power, which she could not exercise without possible bloodshed between the Hawaiian police force and the U.S. troops. Under international law, the Liliʻuokalani assignment, is a treaty, and under United States law, it is considered a sole executive agreement that does not require ratification from the U.S. Senate or approval of Congress to have the force and effect of a treaty. Sole-executive agreements bind successor Presidents for the faithful execution.

Lease—A grant of land to a person from either someone with the fee-simple or life estate for a fixed term of years.

Legal fiction—An assumption made by a court that something occurred which, in fact, did not, but is contrived in order to allow a court to resolve a matter before it. Legal fictions are not supposed to violate the law, but rather used to equitably resolve a dispute or matter that has come before the court.

Legislative power—The power of a branch of government to enact law. According to article 45 of the Hawaiian Constitution, "The Legislative power of the Three Estates of this Kingdom is vested in the King, and the Legislative Assembly; which Assembly shall consist of the Nobles appointed by the King, and of the Representatives of the People, sitting together."

Lord—A feudal superior.

Maika—Stone used in the ancient Hawaiian game of bowling.

Martial law—A law exercised over the civilian population of domestic territory of the United States through U.S. military forces as necessity requires, e.g. the martial law imposed over the civilian population of the rebel States of the Union during the American Civil War. According to the United States Army Field Manual 27-10, "the most prominent distinction between military government and martial law is that the former is generally exercised in the territory of, or territory formerly occupied by, a hostile belligerent and is subject to restraints imposed by the international law of belligerent occupation, while the latter is invoked only in domestic territory, the local government and inhabitants of which are not treated or recognized as belligerents, and is governed solely by the domestic law of the United States.

Military government—A government established by the United States military in a foreign country that administers the international laws of occupation and the laws of the occupied country or state. According to U.S. Army Field Manual 27-10, "Military government is an accepted concept in the law of the United States, and the limits placed upon its exercise are prescribed by the international law of belligerent occupation. Other countries exercise jurisdiction in occupied areas through types of administration analogous to military government even though they may be designated by other names."

Minister Plenipotentiary—The head of a diplomatic mission in a foreign country called a Legation.

Mōʻī—King, sovereign, monarch, majesty, ruler, queen.

Mosaic law—The laws of the Pentateuch and the Ten Commandments given to Moses in the bible.

Nationality—The status of belonging to a particular country or state, through citizenship, *i.e.* the nationality of a person, or property, *i.e.* the nationality of a ship.

Natural rights—Basic rights laid down by nature and God, which no government can deny. Natural rights grew out of the medieval doctrines of natural law that saw man as natural beings under God. The 1839 Declaration of Rights stated these rights to be "life, limb, liberty, freedom from oppression; the earnings of his hands and the productions of his mind."

Occupation—see Law of Occupation

Organic law—The fundamental law or system of laws that forms the foundation of a government. A constitution is a form of organic law for a country or state.

Palapala—Literally translated as a document of any kind, which formerly meant to learn to read and write.

Penal Code—An organized collection of criminal laws for a society published in book form that is intended for easy access by the populace.

Pono—Goodness, uprightness, morality, moral qualities, correct or proper procedure, excellence.

Privy Council—A body of individuals appointed by a Monarch to give him confidential and private advise on affairs of state. According to the Hawaiian Civil Code, "It shall be the duty of every Privy Counselor; (1) To advise the King according to the best of his knowledge and discretion; (2) To advise for the King's honor and the good of the public, without partiality through friendship, love, reward, fear or favor; (2) Finally, to avoid corruption—and to observe, keep, and do all that a good and true counselor ought to observe, keep, and do to his Sovereign."

Ratification—The approval of the principal of an act of its agent where the agent lacked authority to legally bind the principal. In international law, the principal is the government and the agent is its diplomat. Under article II, clause 2, of the U.S. Constitution, states that the President "shall have

Power, by and with the Advice and Consent of the Senate, to make Treaties, provided two thirds of the Senators present concur." According to Hawaiian law, treaties are ratified by the Monarch by and with the advice of the Cabinet Council. According to article 42 of the Hawaiian Constitution, "No act of the King shall have any effect unless it be countersigned by a Minister, who by that signature makes himself responsible."

Regency—A person or body of officials that represent a kingdom during the minority, absence, insanity, or other disability of a Monarch. According to article 33 of the Hawaiian Constitution, "It shall be lawful for the King at any time when he may be about to absent himself from the Kingdom, to appoint a Regent or Council of Regency, who shall administer the Government in His name; and likewise the King may, by His last Will and Testament, appoint a Regent or Council of Regency to administer the Government during the minority of any Heir to the Throne: and should a Sovereign decease, leaving a Minor Heir, and having made no last Will and Testament, the Cabinet Council at the time of such decease shall be a Council of Regency, until the Legislative Assembly, which shall be called immediately, may be assembled, and the Legislative Assembly immediately that it is assembled shall proceed to choose by ballot, a Regent or Council of Regency, who shall administer the Government in the name of the King, and exercise all the Powers which are Constitutionally vested in the King, until he shall have attained the age of eighteen years, which age is declared to be the Legal Majority of such Sovereign."

Revolution—A complete overthrow of the established government in any country or state by individuals who once held allegiance and subject to its laws. A revolution is distinguished from revolt, which is an attempt to overthrow an established government.

Self-determination—A principle in international law that nations have the right to freely determine their political status and pursue their economic, social and cultural development. The international community first used the term after World War I where the former territorial possessions of the Ottoman Empire and Germany were assigned to individual member countries or states of the League of Nations for administration as Mandate territories. The function of the administration of these territories was to facilitate the process of self-determination whereby these territories would achieve full recognition as an independent and sovereign state. After World War II, territories of Japan and Italy were added and assigned to be administered individual member countries or states of the United Nations, being the successor of the League of Nations, and were called Trust territories. Also added to these territories were territories held by all other members of the United Nations and called Non-self-governing territories. Unlike the Mandate and Trust territories, they were not assigned to other member countries or states for administration, but remained under the original colonial authority who reported yearly to the United Nations on the status of these territories. Self-determination for Non-self-governing territories had three options: total incorporation into the colonial country or state, free association with the colonial country or state, or complete independence from the colonial country or state. Self-determination for indigenous peoples does not include independence and is often referred to as self-determination within the country or state they reside in.

Separation of powers doctrine—A division of governance of a country under a written constitution that separates and makes distinct the three branches of government—legislative, executive, and judicial. The Legislative Assembly is vested with the legislative power to make law; the Monarch is vested with the executive power to enforce and administer law; and the Judiciary is vested with the judicial power to adjudicate disputes under the law.

Sole Executive Agreement—An agreement made between the President of the United States and another country that does not require ratification from the United States Senate or approval of the Congress to have the force and effect of a treaty under U.S. constitutional law.

Sovereignty—Supreme authority exercised over a particular territory. In international law, it is the supreme and absolute authority exercised through a government, being independent of any other sovereignty. Sovereignty, being authority, is distinct from government, which is the physical body that exercises the authority. Therefore, a government can be overthrown, but the sovereignty remains.

Sovereignty movement—A political movement of a wide range of groups in the Hawaiian Islands that seek to exercise self-determination under international law as a Non-self-governing unit, or to exercise internal self-determination under the 2007 United Nations Declaration on the Rights of Indigenous Peoples. The commonality of these various groups is that their political platforms are based on aboriginal Hawaiian identity and culture and use of the United Nations term indigenous people. The movement presumes that the Hawaiian Kingdom and its sovereignty were overthrown by the United States January 17th 1893, and therefore the movement is seeking to reclaim that sovereignty through de-colonization. The movement does not operate on the presumption of continuity of the Hawaiian Kingdom as an independent state and the law of occupation, but rather on the aspiration of becoming an independent state or some form of internal self-determination within the laws of the United States.

Treaty—An agreement or contract between two or more governments of independent states formally signed by authorized commissioners, ratified by both governments, and an exchange of ratifications that will execute the contract.

Unicameral legislature—A legislative body with one house, *i.e.* Legislative Assembly comprised of both appointed Nobles and elected Representatives sitting together in one house. According to article 45 of the Hawaiian Constitution, "The Legislative power of the Three Estates of this Kingdom is vested in the King, and the Legislative Assembly; which Assembly shall consist of the Nobles appointed by the King, and of the Representatives of the People, sitting together."

Vassal—(in the feudal system) a person granted the use of land, in return for rendering homage, fealty, and usually military service or its equivalent to a lord or other superior; feudal tenant.

INDEX

PEOPLE

ROYALTY & HEADS OF STATE

HISTORICAL OR POLITICAL FIGURES

LAW PRACTITIONERS & SCHOLARS

HAWAIIAN KINGDOM GOVERNMENT

ABOUT THE PŪʻĀ FOUNDATION

Pūʻā: The process of feeding, nourishing & strengthening. Let's learn together, work together, & eat together.

Pūʻā Foundation is a 501(c)(3) non-profit organization that was established in 1996 as part of the apology, redress, and reconciliation initiatives of the United Church of Christ for its complicity in the overthrow of the Hawaiian monarchy. Through pūʻā—the process of feeding, nourishing and strengthening—we can embark on the journey of healing and forgiveness, moving toward the emergence of an enlightened and empowered unified community.

In reconciling what has past and forging a promising future, we aim to facilitate opportunities for a deeper and clearer understanding of the historical, cultural, spiritual and economic impacts of the overthrow. We do so by engaging community dialogue, and encouraging public discourse to transform a legacy of hurt into one of hope for all of Hawaiʻi's people.

To learn more go to *www.puafoundation.org*. We welcome your support - contributions of time, talents and treasures are most appreciated.

ABOUT THE AUTHOR

Dr. Keanu Sai received his Ph.D. in political science from the University of Hawaiʻi at Manoa in 2008 specializing in international law, state sovereignty, international laws of occupation, United States constitutional law, and Hawaiian constitutional law. His research specifically addressed the legal and political history of the Hawaiian Islands since the eighteenth century to the present. Dr. Sai has authored several law journal articles on the topic of the continuity of Hawaiian Kingdom as a sovereign state, and served as lead agent for the Hawaiian Kingdom in arbitration proceedings before the Permanent Court of Arbitration, The Hague, Netherlands, in Lance Larsen v. Hawaiian Kingdom (1999-2001). Dr. Sai currently teaches Hawaiian Studies at Windward Community College on the Island of Oʻahu.